A YOUNG CHILD EXPERIENCES

GOODYEAR EDUCATION SERIES
Theodore W. Hipple, Editor

A YOUNG CHILD EXPERIENCES

Activities for Teaching and Learning

Sandra Nina Kaplan
Jo Ann Butom Kaplan
Sheila Kunishima Madsen
Bette Taylor Gould

Goodyear Publishing Company, Inc.
Pacific Palisades, California

Louie Neiheisel, *designer and art director*
Sherri Butterfield, *project editor*
Sheila Madsen, *illustrator*
Gail Weingart, *supervising editor*

Library of Congress Cataloging in Publication Data
Main entry under title:

A Young child experiences.

(Goodyear education series)
1. Creative activities and seat work. 2. Education
Primary—Curricula. I. Kaplan, Sandra Nina.
LB1537.Y65   372.1'9   74-17833
ISBN 0-87620-993-2 pkb.

Copyright © 1975 by Goodyear Publishing Company, Inc.,
Pacific Palisades, California

Library of Congress Catalog Card Number: 74-17833

ISBN: 0-87620-993-2

Y-9932-8

Current Printing (last number):
10 9 8 7 6 5 4 3 2 1

Printed in the United States of America

To Kent and Key, Sol and Muriel, Bill and Grace, Mary and Michael

CONTENTS

Note

See page 168 for a complete list of the pages on which task cards and worksheets appear, the activity to which they correspond, and the page on which that activity is described.

Key to Symbols

A corresponding task card or game to cut out and back with heavier paper or laminate for repeated use can be found at the back of the book.

A corresponding worksheet to be duplicated can be found at the back of the book.

INTRODUCTION

Father: What did you learn at school today, Kenny?

Kenny: Noth'n.

Mother: Tell your father what you did at school today, Kenny.

Kenny: Oh! . . . I built a robot and made ice cream, and played with the dinosaur bones, and painted a picture and made up a story, and . . . and . . .

For a young child, "doing" consumes much of his time, attention, and energy. Although he may not consciously connect his involvement in "doing" with "learning," it is through his many experiences, both in and out of school, that he continually adds to his own framework of knowledge.

A young child's school experiences can be his work, his play, his teacher, and his curriculum. A child's involvement in an activity or situation created for or by him is the catalyst for learning. Learning evolves naturally from the things children do. The purpose of a classroom program of experiential learning is to capitalize on all the possibilities that are a natural outgrowth of what the child has done. Such a program uses planned and spontaneous situations and activities to encourage the child to discover and accumulate knowledge about himself and the world in which he lives. Experiential learning is learning *from* something rather than being taught *about* something; it is discovering by oneself rather than being told.

LEARNING IS ACTIVE INVOLVEMENT.
In an experiential learning program where the child is an active participant in the learning process, he is both uncovering and receiving information. His physical and mental absorption satisfy a need and create an interest in learning. His own interests, needs, and abilities become the factors that determine *what* is being learned. Play, and the exploration and experimentation that accompany it, is the condition that determines *how* the learning occurs.

EXPERIENCES ARE THE CURRICULUM. Experiences, and the sharing and questioning of them, become the curriculum for the child. The potential for naturally and meaningfully integrating any facet of learning into an experience should be considered when appropriate to the child. The learning of fundamental skills should be a part of the activities of an experience. The teacher's awareness of when these skills can be most appropriately introduced and extended and her ability to stimulate the child's interest are necessary. Knowing when and how to facilitate further learnings from an experience is the major responsibility of the teacher.

THERE ARE DIFFERENT QUALITIES AND TYPES OF EXPERIENCES. Not all types of experiences may be necessary or valuable to all students. Planned experiences can fulfill a particular need for a particular time and child. Although many clues for providing different experiences will come from an understanding of who the child is, there will also be experiences that teachers will want every child to have. Teacher-structured experiences are as valid as student-determined ones.

Many experiences cannot be objectively evaluated. Some experiences contain value in the potential they have for motivating and stimulating learning which will be used at another time and place; therefore, the teacher must recognize that experiences offer secondary and subtle learnings which may not be readily apparent. The child's own unique mental structure, needs, and interests ultimately determine the type and quality of the experience and the learnings that result from it.

EACH EXPERIENCE GENERATES NEW EXPERIENCES AND LEARNING POSSIBILITIES. Each experience creates opportunities for the development of new experiences. What a child gains from one experience can be used as a resource and reference for planning another experience. Learnings are continually being linked to experiences in unique patterns or sequences to form the child's background of knowledge. Each pattern differs according to the individual nature of the learner.

Glossary of Terms

With the recognition that words and their meanings are dependent on situations and speakers, it is necessary to provide a frame of reference for the interpretations and understanding of terms as they are used in the context of this book.

Affective learning: development of self-concept and understanding of emotions as they relate to oneself and others

Child-centered curriculum— a program: relying on who the child is and what he is doing as the basis for designing and presenting learning activities

Curriculum: every experience the child has had both inside and outside the school setting

Discovery: the process of finding out for oneself, preferably through play, firsthand investigation, and experimentation

Environmental learning: using the real world as a resource for learning

Experiential learning: the process of learning by doing

Individualized instruction: a classroom program based on children's needs, with varied possibilities for learning, as well as varied opportunities for students to design and choose their own learning experiences

Junk: a variety of expendable objects, recycled by children as materials for expressing and illustrating

Manipulatives: materials that necessitate handling, moving, touching to assist children in learning by doing

Multi-age grouping: placement of students in groups according to multiple criteria which may include chronological age, grade level and interest, need and/or ability assessments

Play: planned or spontaneous activities children enjoy and choose to do on their own

Self-selection: a process allowing students opportunities to make choices of any or all of the experiences offered them: the task to be performed, the method of learning, the mode of expression, the time and place to complete the task

Structure: underlying outline or organizational pattern for providing learning possibilities to children

Talking: verbal interacting or describing of people, places, and things in order to better understand the world, and the individuals and events in it

Teacher: a person who helps learning by arranging for learning experiences, providing a caring, supportive atmosphere for learning, and interacting with students by initiating and extending learning from their experiences

Writing: using and practicing written symbols in order to communicate and retain one's own ideas, impressions, and experiences

**Dimensions of a Program
for Young Children**

Children:
Communicate,
Play, Move, Feel

THE ENVIRONMENT

A VARIETY OF MATERIALS
commercial, natural,
recycled,
junk

CONSTANTLY BEING
CHANGED...
by children, teacher, parents,
community

INVITES PLAY, DISCOVERY,
AND EXPERIMENTATION.

A VARIETY OF SPACES...
quiet and noisy, big and
small, alone and together,

DISPLAY PLACES

MULTIPLE ENVIRONMENTS
inside the classroom
outside the classroom
and beyond the classroom.

THE TEACHER

accepting, encouraging,
caring

observing, inquiring,
assessing

asking rather than telling

trusting in a child's ability to
learn and make decisions

knowing about child growth
and development

acting as a partner
in learning

THE STRUCTURE

student decision making

informal and formal
learning activities

ways for children to
evaluate themselves and
their learning

alone, small group, total
group experiences

broad range of learning
possibilities

encouragement of mobility,
talking, interaction

1.
TEACHER EXPERIENCES

Creating an Environment for Learning

The classroom environment is a reflection of the teacher's philosophy about children and learning, and the expectations she holds for both. Consideration of these factors, as well as an ongoing assessment of the children, determines how the classroom will be organized and managed and what type of learning activities and materials will be placed within it.

BECAUSE CHILDREN NEED FREEDOM TO MOVE... the classroom environment should be organized into activity areas. The division of the room into areas can be accomplished by partitioning off space with screens, boxes, tables, and pieces of cardboard. Space can be obtained by abolishing the idea of a desk for each child and by moving some of these desks into learning areas or completely out of the room.

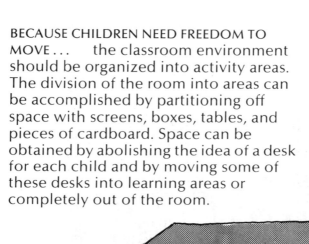

BECAUSE CHILDREN CAN DIRECT THEIR OWN LEARNING ... the classroom environment should display materials in a way that makes them readily accessible to children. Supplies housed in labeled areas, worksheets labeled and ordered in boxes, cartons, and bookshelves, and students' work projects and papers in individual storage bins are a few ways that allow children to work independently in the classroom. Centers displaying a collection of specific activities and resources enable children to self-select from an array of learning possibilities. A classroom program that allows children to schedule some of their own time and to select from teaching/learning alternatives reinforces the concept that children share the responsibility for their learning.

BECAUSE CHILDREN HAVE SPECIFIC NEEDS AND INTERESTS ... the classroom environment should have a wide variety and range of learning activities and materials to which children can be directed, or from which children can choose. Opportunities for self-initiated individual study projects should be scheduled into the program and should be facilitated by small group and individual meetings with the teacher.

BECAUSE CHILDREN ARE PARTNERS IN THE
LEARNING PROCESS . . .   the classroom
task of developing and collecting
materials and activities, and placing
them in the environment should be
shared by students and teacher. The care
of materials and general order of the
classroom are also responsibilities that
should be shared by all members of the
class.

BECAUSE CHILDREN NEED TO DEVELOP
AFFECTIVELY AS WELL AS COGNITIVELY . . .
the classroom atmosphere must value
and allow for individual differences by
encouraging independent study,
presenting many ways of illustrating
learning outcomes, and accepting
multiple forms of personal expression.
Attention to the various levels of
emotional maturity and social skills
attained by each child will help teachers
determine the amount of responsibility
he can assume. The teacher evaluates
children in relationship to who they are
and encourages children to evaluate
themselves in relationship to
individually defined criteria.

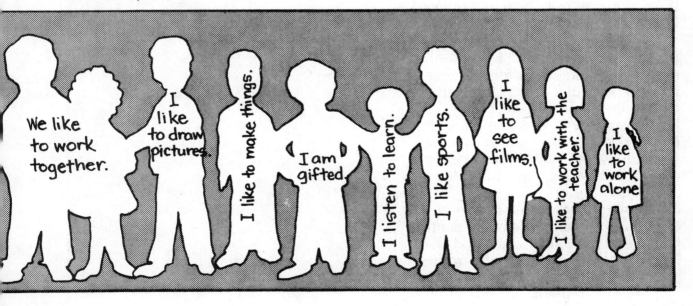

Organizing Activities

Using Activities Individually

Each of the collections of related activities in this book can be used as an individual experience. Sometimes these activities are arranged separately in the room because of space and material limitations. A teacher's particular program of instruction and teaching style may influence the manner in which she uses these activities. The teacher may wish to use single activities in the room for small group lessons. It is important to label the activities and to introduce them to students so that the locale, time, and materials needed to work with the activities are understood.

Learning Centers

A learning center is a collection of activities developed around a topic, theme, skill, or subject. Learning centers provide students with activities at varying levels of difficulty and complexity. They cater to individual learning styles by including activities structured to appeal to the different senses. One reason for using learning centers is to place the activities in the classroom environment so that students can work independently or in groups at the center and thereby direct their own learning for some time during the school day. A learning center therefore functions as a "teacher" by presenting, reinforcing, and extending learning about a particular topic. Unlike the classroom teacher, however, the learning center is not self-sufficient and is dependent on the teacher to ensure its workability. In using learning centers, the teacher assumes the multiple responsibilities of

Initiating— The teacher determines what the learning center should include and plans for methods of introducing it and scheduling students to use it.

Interacting— The teacher presents group lessons at the center and arranges for individual conferences with students to discuss their experiences at the center. The teacher adopts techniques to determine when and how to intervene with the student's experiences in order to aid in clarifying, reinforcing, and extending learning.

Evaluating— The teacher continually checks on the center's appeal and usability for children. Some activities may need revising, or replacement with new ones in order to meet the objectives set up by the teacher and students.

Although learning centers are a complete unit, the various activities within them can be used by the teacher as group lessons or individual assignments. A single set of activities from a center can be placed within the environment for students to use on a self-selected or scheduled basis.

Here is a pattern learning centers can follow to make them functional and appropriate for students.

Pattern for a Learning Center

Develop	Collect	Display	Present	Evaluate
Select a topic, subject, skill, or interest as the basis for creating activities	Locate all references and resources about the topic, skill, or interest: realia study prints filmstrips records books	Section off an area in the classroom Arrange the materials using: cardboard bulletin boards peg boards boxes tables chart racks plastic bins	Introduce activities Give directions on how to use materials Schedule times for using the center	Develop a record-keeping instrument for student's or teacher's use. Provide ways for children to share products
Structure activities to include: ways to receive information— listening observing experimenting researching	Gather all materials to be used for: building writing drawing modeling sorting	Label items Place signs and directions around center	Schedule individual conferences Encourage students to act as teachers for the center	
ways to apply information— making products designing models filling in worksheets putting together puzzles acting out scenes playing games writing stories matching objects	Set up supplies: scissors paper pencils marking pens glue stapler paper punch crayons chalk string	Indicate space for working Allow for display of children's work	Plan for ways children can add activities to the center Teach group lessons at the center	

Getting Children to the Experiences

There are many ways to introduce and direct young chidren to the learning possibilities arranged within the environment. All of these ways have some elements in common: they present alternatives to children; they provide a procedure by which children may select an experience; they indicate some method by which numbers of children and time zones for activities are organized.

Some Ways to Start the Day

Morning Meeting
The teacher meets with the total class to discuss the day's events, inform the students of the things to be accomplished, hand out needed or requested materials, and provide for individuals and groups of children to sign up for various activities. Sign-ups can be handled by having the teacher or children write their selections under activity headings on a chalkboard, chart, or individual schedule.

General Activity Block of Time
The teacher discusses with the children the activities in which they will participate during the first work time block of the day. While the children work, the teacher meets with individuals or small groups of students to individualize their plans for the remainder of the day.

Student Scheduling
The teacher designs some form of scheduling device for students to use to record their choices for the day. Young children may need to use pictures, symbols, colors, or other simple methods for recording choices without a great deal of teacher supervision.

Open Choice
The teacher has discussed the day's events with the children at the close of the previous day. Children come into the classroom and freely select their learning activity and begin to work. As the day progresses the children move from area to area with the teacher's assistance and some formal attendance in large and small groups.

Daily Class Schedules
The teacher outlines the day's schedule on the chalkboard or a chart. She reviews the schedule with the children and presents some type of signal to help them know when to change from one selected activity to another.

Helping Children with the Experiences

Intervention as opposed to interference is the key to moving from manipulation to other levels of learning. With experience, the aware teacher will become increasingly skilled at choosing the time for intervention. Either the child's questions or his performance will determine this timing, or the teacher's perceptions of the child's needs will suggest a point of intervention. Whenever intervention seems appropriate, the teacher must be prepared to ask questions which present alternative possibilities for activity, research, thinking, and expression. By intervening the teacher is recognizing that the child's manipulative experiences are beginning points for a whole series of learning stages and that intervention is an invitation for the child to stretch into these stages.

Questions to Ask:

1. How could you use this? How many different ways?
2. How does this work?
3. Have you thought about looking at this?
4. What else could you do to show this?
5. How did you figure this out?
6. Could you show someone else how to do this?

Record Keeping and Reporting

The kinds of learning activities and how well they have been accomplished are the essence of what teacher and student need to record and report. Everything a child does need not be reported, and the student as well as the teacher should determine what to include. The child's concept of himself as an individual and member of a group and his needs for affective learning will play a part in this determination. Records should be easy to keep, and evaluation methods should be meaningful if they are to be deserving of the time spent on them. Reporting practices for young children should emphasize conferences and comments rather than number or letter grades.

Records should be maintained and evaluations made to

- determine further learning possibilities
- assess individual growth
- determine the personal and intellectual characteristics of the child
- involve parents in the learning process
- plan for materials and resources to enrich the program
- assist the child in defining who he is

Teacher Recording Instruments

STUDENT FOLDERS   A manila folder is labeled for each child. A dittoed insert with headings for date, observation, and plans is used by the teacher to record information about the child. These folders can be passed on to other teachers and can be used as the basis for parent and student conferences.

INDEX CARD FILE   A card is labeled for each child. Categories for different skill areas, needs, and interests are identified on dividers. The teacher writes notes about the child on his card and files the card behind the appropriate divider.

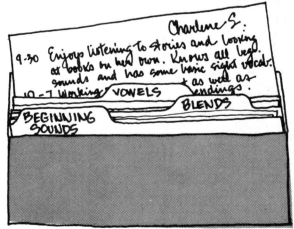

PICTURE RECORDS   Photographs are taken of children at work or of projects they have completed. The pictures can be placed in a scrapbook which has a page for each child. Comments can be written by the teacher or dictated by the child on the page. At various times during the year, the child can take his page home as a means of reporting to parents.

Student Recording Instruments

TREASURE BOXES   Each child uses a box to keep the samples of work he treasures. The boxes can be brought up to share with the teacher at conference time. The teacher can add notes about the child's work to the treasure box. Boxes can be taken home and given to parents as evidence of what the child has accomplished and values at school.

TRIANGLE NOTES   The teacher dittoes off a large triangle with the words "Today some of my activities have been . . ." on it. The child can dictate or write in the remainder of the sentence. The triangle is sent home to parents at the end of the day. It might also include a note requesting a parent response, thus encouraging home-school communication.

STUDENT LETTER   Children are given copies of a dittoed letter to fill out at the end of the school day. They color in pictures of what they have done during the day and circle what they enjoyed most. This type of record keeping and reporting instrument encourages parent and student interaction.

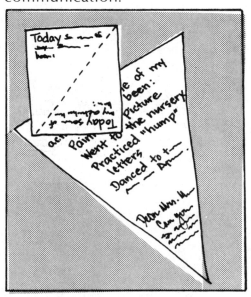

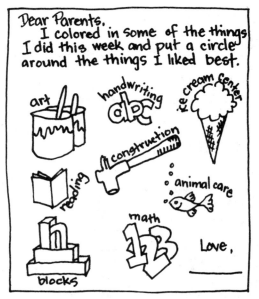

The Teacher's Day

The teacher's schedule is a composite of things that must be attended to during the day. Regardless of format, it must include time for

- working with individual students
- teaching small groups of students
- announcing and scheduling the day's events with the total class
- enjoying the children at work and play
- observing, questioning, and listening as students are involved in activities
- meeting with people who support the classroom program
- preparing and developing activities and collecting materials

---

Reminders: – Call John's mother about collecting junk materials
– Reserve school oven
– Set up reading corner for reptile group
– Meet with aide at 3 p.m.

9:00-9:30 MORNING MEETING

* Sign up for special events
9:30-10:30 Museum resource person - Mrs. Jones - Reptiles - 10 children
12:20 Mrs. Campbell - group to make brownies during lunchtime
1:00-2:30 Walk to nursery with Mrs. Ames: Tommy, Sara, Mark, Danny, Hank, Tamara

* <u>MUSTS FOR DAY</u> 1) a writing product 2) one measuring activity 3) Happy Birthday Center
* Board sign-ups <u>Blocks</u> <u>Junk Center</u> <u>Me and other Creatures Center</u>
4 children 6 4
* Meet with a group (6-7 children) to work with balance scale

---

9:30-11:00 ACTIVITY PERIOD

Above activities
After Balance Scale groups:
CONFERENCES – Dave on robot project
– Sally and Jim on aquarium project
– Louise – ballet mobile
Float & observe: especially look for children who need color recognition help
Check on Loren to see what she's done so far

11:00-12:00 TOTAL GROUP

<u>Outside</u>: Body Parts Orchestra - use <u>Sorcerer's Apprentice</u>
       * get phonograph and records

Sharing and discussing of morning's activities

12:00-12:45 LUNCH

12:20 - Carol's mother in to make brownies with cooking group
      * Larry to pick up supplies from refrigerator

    5th grade boys to help with kickball game

12:45-1:00

Do class graph on papers picked up on playground during lunchtime

* Nursery walk group - Mrs. Ames
      * remember: camera
                graph paper
                pens

1:00-1:30 SKILL GROUPS

Blends group at carpet area

Other children: choice time at centers
      * Marcia to help at Junk Center
      * Bob and Paul - outside measuring work

1:30-2:15

Listen to children read - at their choice - Reading Corner
    * Be sure to listen to John and Toby - note observations on
                              their reading cards
    * <u>2:00</u> - Group to library to check out books

2:15-2:30 CLEAN UP

<u>Meet at carpet</u>
    - Share brownies
    - Distribute junk collection bags to go home
    - Remind children to check their mailboxes for notes
  * Set hamster trap
    - Remind Paul to return microscope

School Supports

The school is just one facet in the total environmental structure that nurtures the young child's learning. To the extent that the school integrates itself with other resources to accommodate a young child's learning, it is even more effective in fulfilling the child's learning needs. Although the school may be recognized as the focal point for educating the child, it is necessary to realize that learning is continuously taking place wherever and with whomever the child interacts. Acceptance of this fact mandates the inclusion of other people and places in the school curriculum and the exclusion of the concept that learning is contained within the boundaries of the school site.

The first step in expanding the learning environment is to incorporate additional personnel into the school and/or classroom.

Working with Aides

Regardless of whether aides are paid or volunteer their time, it is important that the type of school or classroom tasks they are to perform and the expectations for their performance be clearly stated if they are to be used to maximum effectiveness. Helping the aides see their relevancy to a young child's learning process may influence the level of commitment and responsibility with which they will carry out their roles. Before instituting an aide program,

- Allow potential aides to personally assess their strengths, weaknesses, and interests in relationship to the types of school and classroom positions that are open and which they, in turn, could most satisfactorily and comfortably fill.
- Stipulate on a daily, weekly, or permanent basis exactly what the school or classroom task entails and why the task is important for children.
- Plan for a preservice program which instructs aides in the characteristics of children and the basic ways of assisting and interacting with children. If necessary, provide training in the most effective methods of teaching a particular skill or subject.
- Schedule ongoing sessions for aides to discuss and question their roles with other aides, other staff members, and with the teacher they are assisting.
- Provide aides with the opportunity to make suggestions about certain aspects of the classroom so that a sense of contribution, belonging, and partnership can be established.
- Acknowledge the differences in responsibility and role assignments between the paraprofessional and the professional to establish a comfortable working relationship.
- Plan, as necessary, for teachers to develop effective methods in the use of aides in the classroom.

Working with Parents

Positive parent relationships with the school help the child see and understand the value placed on learning. Ideally, the educational structure should be considered an extension of the home and community. Continuous opportunities for the school and home, and the parents and teachers to reinforce and support each other must be planned, articulated, encouraged, and most important, expected. Perhaps the major reason many parents are uninvolved in the school is the school's inability to show parents how involvement can and should take place.

STIMULATING PARENT INTEREST   A complete program to enlist parents in an active school support program should include what needs to be done, why involvement is necessary, benefits derived from involvement, and the responsibility of sharing the child's learning process and progress. Parents can be contacted through the mail, meetings, posters, and student letters. When these more traditional methods for contacting parents are ignored, new and creative ways need to be tried, such as:

- Saturday or Sunday morning work day to develop some new activities or equipment for the classroom
- Total class visits to a child's home or yard during the school day
- Bus trips scheduled for parents for visiting other schools to observe programs and facilities
- Simulation classroom experiences for parents, during which they actually use the classroom environment

ORIENTING PARENTS FOR INVOLVEMENT   A well-organized series of meetings to facilitate home and school support may include such topics as:

- Questions to ask teachers during a conference
- Materials and experiences at home which augment the classroom program
- How to measure your child's learning progress
- Developmental characteristics and needs of children
- How to work in your child's classroom
- Tasks to fulfill classroom needs
- Things to gather at home to send to the classroom
- Tasks parents can do at home for the teacher or classroom
- Reproducing and developing classroom learning materials
- Being a resource person by sharing a personal talent or interest

ATTENDING TO PARENTS   A schedule indicating when and how needed support services can be executed should be set up. In addition, a continuous system of communicating with parents on an informal and formal basis solidifies the home-school relationship. Besides the customary conferences, letters, and notes, a bag or container can be sent home with the child which contains various items to share, discuss, and use at home with his parents.

Games, projects, and products of a child's activities are helpful to parents in becoming familiar with school or class learning experiences.

RECOGNIZING PARENT SUPPORT   It is important to recognize parents who offer to help. This recognition can take the form of inviting those with particular expertise to serve as a resource to the class, or it can be accomplished through teas, letters of commendation, and certificates of service. As with children, the reinforcement of a task well done heightens the possibility of its being continued and valued.

In order to utilize parents effectively as classroom volunteers, teachers need to ask:

- What tasks can be done for children which could not otherwise be accomplished or provided?
- Can Mrs. Smith (or any class parent) be used in class without jeopardizing or hindering her child's school experience?
- How can orientation, discussions, and assignments of parent volunteers best be scheduled?
- Where can needed tasks for the class, individual, or small groups of children take place?
- How can parents' personal characteristics and professional skills be assessed in order to use them most effectively without creating problems or concerns for the school, staff, or children?
- Which tasks and methods of contact will help shy, culturally different, or hostile parents feel comfortable and secure as volunteers?

Working with the Community

Because the community is a component of the total learning environment, an assessment of what is available, how and when it can be used, and who can be contacted for its use must be made. The commercial and professional establishments and agencies within a community often have provisions for services to the schools and individuals or groups of children. These need to be explored and recorded. Files of such resources can be developed by parents, students, and staff members for use within the school. The use of community resources need not be confined to school hours. Many community services can be utilized before and after the school day or on weekends, thereby offering excellent opportunities to involve parents in their child's learning. As teachers work to develop their individual class, grade, or school curriculum, it is imperative that they include community supports in the scope of learning possibilities.

Some activities to encourage community involvement are:

- Conduct a yellow page telephone directory search to find out what and how establishments and agencies can offer assistance to the school
- Contact senior citizen organizations to develop a Grandparents Club to serve as school resources and helpers
- Find out when community workers, such as gardeners, street cleaners, and repairmen, will be in the neighborhood for class observations and interviews

- Make signs for billboards and create posters for windows to solicit resources for the school
- Call local colleges or universities for the possible use of personnel and facilities to assist in school programs

2.
JUNK EXPERIENCES

When a child uses junk . . .
he is involved,
he is interested,
he is learning!

Using junk in the classroom capitalizes on the child's innate curiosity about objects in the environment. Junk aids the process of learning and becomes a product of a learning experience. With junk, children play, discover, practice, and learn. Informal play should precede the activities in this chapter. The child's initial motivation and involvement in play are extended into specific learning activities. Play should be a continuous part of the learning process.

A necessary factor in using junk is a classroom atmosphere where students are encouraged to explore and create. Selection of and experimentation with junk are as important as the end product. Using old things in new ways stimulates the child's ability to think creatively, practice problem-solving skills, and develop an awareness of the possibilities of recycling materials.

Collecting Junk

The task of gathering junk is shared by the teacher and the students. Decide together what is needed and how it can be collected. The junk should include both surplus and discarded objects. Commercial, neighborhood, and home sources should be explored. Soliciting and collecting junk are a means of rallying community interest and involvement in the school. The teacher can structure junk gathering as a learning experience. Skills such as matching, classifying, and counting can be reinforced as students collect junk. The students will also be practicing writing and speaking skills as they interact with people.

A beginning junk collection might include...

- wood scraps
- plastics
- carpet scraps and samples
- paper—wallpaper samples, sandpaper scraps
- aluminum—foil, cans, containers
- wire, nails, bolts, washers, screws, nuts
- sticks—ice cream, tongue depressors
- boxes
- old clothes
- appliances
- fabric scraps
- burlap
- foam rubber
- packing stuff
- records
- light bulbs
- coat hangers
- sponges
- cardboard fabric bolts
- ribbon spools
- bones
- inexpensive edibles—sugar cubes, licorice, crackers, candy
- game parts, old toys
- flooring and roofing samples
- cartons—egg, fruit, butter, juice, milk, ice cream

and might be obtained from...

- hardware stores
- factories
- lumber yards
- construction sites
- markets
- gas stations and other repair shops
- garage sales
- trash day
- nurseries
- offices
- hospitals, doctors, dentists

Children collect junk at home. Using a ditto or drawing of a house, they write the name or draw a picture of each junk item in the room where they found it.

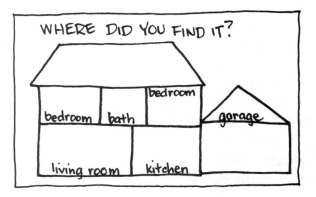

WHERE DID YOU FIND IT?

bedroom bath bedroom

garage

living room kitchen

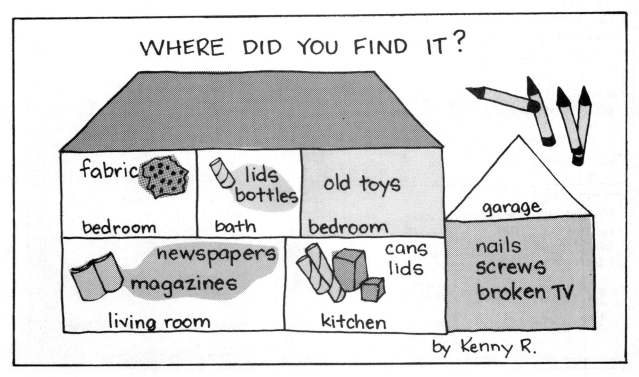

WHERE DID YOU FIND IT?

fabric lids bottles old toys

bedroom bath bedroom

newspapers magazines

living room

cans lids

kitchen

garage

nails screws broken TV

by Kenny R.

Children, individually or as a class, define the terms of an agreement to be made with parents or neighbors in order to collect junk. Agreements are signed by the student and the contributor.

Decorate shopping bags for saving junk. Children distribute them to neighbors or parents with instructions to put them in places where junk is most likely to be found or discarded.

I promise to help you
clean the _____
on _____ for __ hours.

In return I get to keep all
the junk I find.

_____
_____

I promise to help you
clean the _garage_
on _Sunday_ for _2_ hours.

In return I get to keep all
the junk I find. Chris
Mrs. Evans

SAVE
JUNK
FOR
ROOM 10
Return this bag to Andy.

Children search the neighborhood for junk. They complete a graph using pictures, symbols, or colors in the squares to indicate the location and the quantity of junk found.

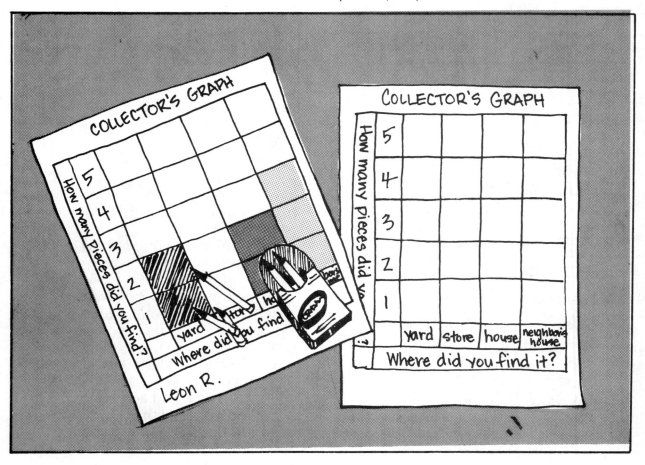

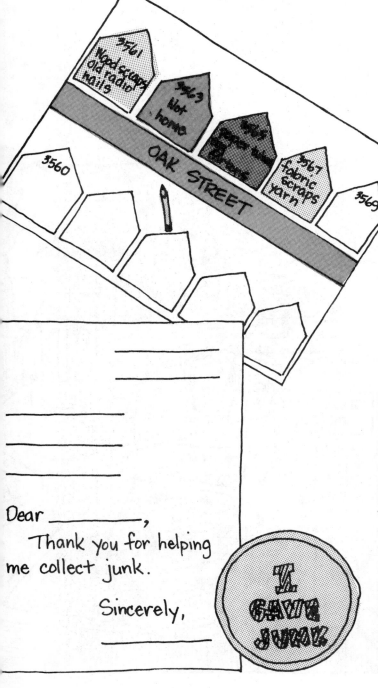

Each child has an area to walk in the neighborhood in order to collect junk. He takes with him a dittoed outline of houses on which he records such things as the address, the number of people living there, whether the people were home, and the type of junk he received. When all the children have brought back their outlines, they may be put together to show a map of the neighborhood. Each neighbor who contributes junk is given an I GAVE JUNK sticker designed by the child or the class. The child also writes the name and address of the person on a dittoed thank-you note. This gives practice in writing numerals, capitals, abbreviations, etc.

Storing Junk

Some system for sorting and labeling junk and making it available to students must be developed. Such a system might be based on categories such as size, type, material, or color, or on intended use. Included in the junk storage area should be tools, such as hammers, saws, staplers, scissors, and glue, which enable the students to work with the junk.

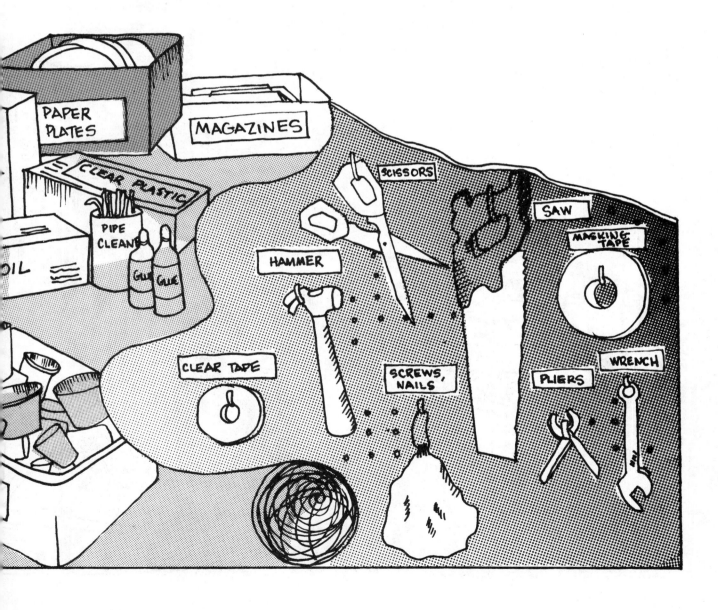

Task Cards

Junk activity task cards are placed individually or in sets with an assortment of gathered junk. The type of junk used should be appropriate for the activity on the card. Sometimes the learning activities necessitate the use of only one large box of assorted junk. At other times the teacher can presort a box of junk to aid children who may have difficulties selecting from a larger collection.

Often task cards stress the learning of a particular skill or subject. Some include techniques for reporting the results of the child's experience so that it can be concretely shown and shared. Although task cards promote independent activity for the student, teachers can use these cards as outlines for lessons in a small group setting or as follow-up for students from a specific teacher-directed lesson.

Placemats

Placemats help students structure learning activity. By placing objects on the mats as directed, students learn a skill or gain experience toward understanding a concept or idea. Although there is an expected learning outcome, students use their own choice of materials.

The format of the placemats enables students to work independently. At a convenient time, the teacher assesses the learning that has taken place by observing the items on the mat and discussing the activity with the child.

Placemats are drawn on paper, fabric, or cardboard which can be rolled up and stored. They may easily be used on table tops or available floor space. Placemats should be large enough to provide space for the manipulation of many sizes of junk materials.

SKILLS

Shape

Make a game board by gluing one junk object on each square. Make a set of cards. On each one draw a portion of the outline of one object on the game board. Players match the cards to the objects they represent. Children can play independently to cover the board. If two or more boards are made, variations of Tic Tac Toe and Bingo can be played. An answer sheet should accompany the game.

Task Cards

Find these crackers.

oval   hexagon   rectangle

triangle   square   circle

Use peanut butter to make a sculpture.

Have some friends make one like yours and have a party.

...t them together ...ke something that ...oves.

Take a picture of it.

crackers
crackers
crackers
crackers

...em on a plate with ...butter.

Serve it to a friend.

large
medium
small

...ogether to ...mething th... in a circle

...to a cir... ...riends.

Placemat

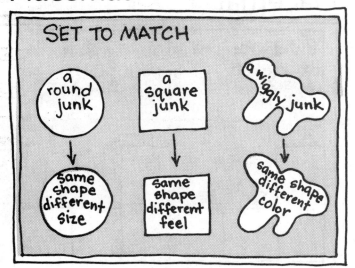

SET TO MATCH

a round junk → same shape different size

a square junk → same shape different feel

a wiggly junk → same shape different color

Placemat

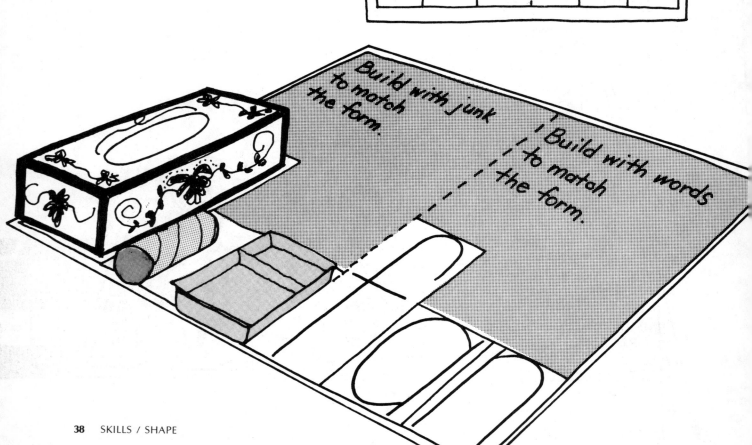

Counting

COUNTING BY 2s

·Build pyramids using one kind of junk such as marshmallows, buttons, paper cups, or egg carton cups. Pyramids can be built in different number patterns such as ones, twos, etc. They can be attached to cardboard. Completed pyramids can be used for counting lessons with small groups or individual children.

ONES PYRAMID

With a shopping list and a bag, a child goes marketing for junk. He takes the junk to a child selected as a checker. The checker, with the shopper, matches the shopping list against the contents of the bag. Another child acts as a stockboy and returns the junk to its original place.

1 doz. beads
½ doz. spools
15 metal things
7 black things
8 pieces of fabric

4
10
3
8

2 + □ = 6

Gather objects which have different numbers of sections. Children find a piece of junk to fill each section. A more difficult adaptation of this activity would be practice in number combinations where the teacher fills in some sections and asks the children how many more are needed to fill the total number of sections in the object.

Task Cards

Pick up a handful of junk in your left hand.

Pick up a handful of junk in your right hand.

GUESS which hand has more.

COUNT to prove your answer.

TELL a friend.

...unt out 10 pieces junk

Put them in groups of 5.

Build something different with each group.

Share it with the class in 10 minutes.

...d get

thing.

...ther

Placemat

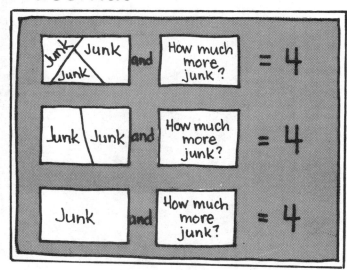

Patterns

Using fruit dividers or egg cartons, paint a pattern for children to complete or copy. A box can also be used. One side is painted, and children complete the other sides in the same pattern.

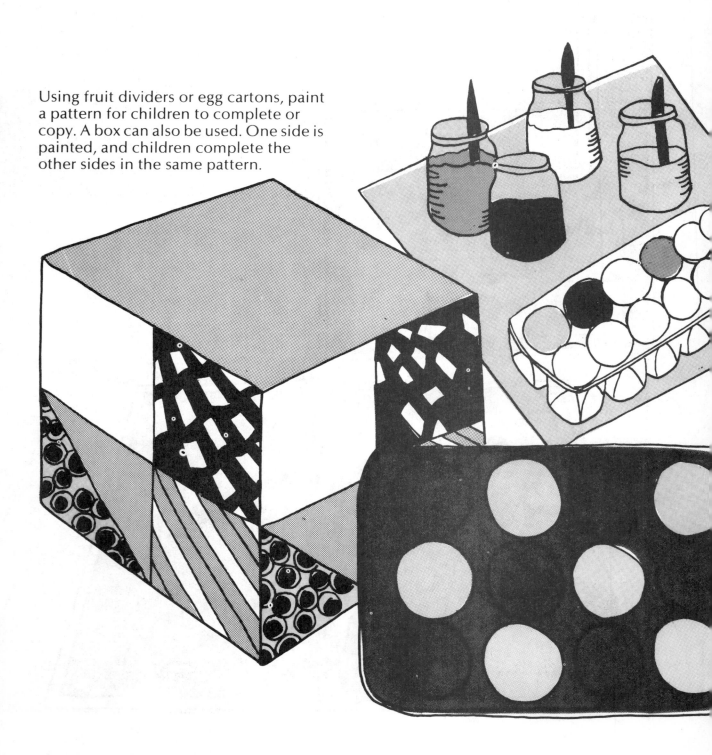

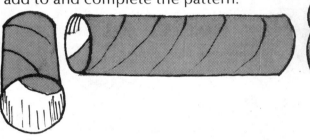

Provide a collection of cardboard tubes of various sizes. Children work in pairs creating patterns for each other to duplicate. Tubes can also be used in a small group. The teacher or a child begins a pattern. Children in the group add to and complete the pattern.

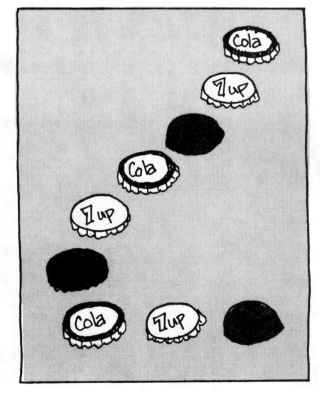

Make a set of cards showing different kinds of patterns which use lids or bottle caps. Children duplicate the patterns by gluing the lids on a piece of cardboard.

Classifying

Label different containers with comparative adjectives. Where possible correlate the quality of the container with the word labeling it. For example, an orange crate could be used as a container labeled with the word ROUGH or WOOD or SQUARE. Children sort directly into the containers from a box containing a random selection of junk.

Print a deck of cards with descriptive words for classifying such as SMOOTH, PLASTIC, BLUE, and ROUND. Children choose any three cards, attach them to containers, and sort junk accordingly. Children can also classify according to multiple qualities such as round and hard, square and soft.

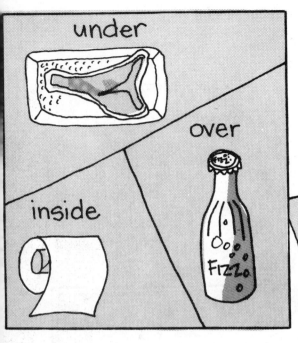

Make charts labeled with the words OVER, UNDER, and INSIDE. Children find junk whose original placement fits one of these categories. The junk is glued onto the chart, and the object it was once part of is drawn in to visually show the relationship of the part to the whole.

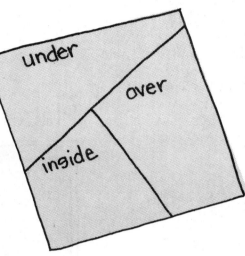

Placemat

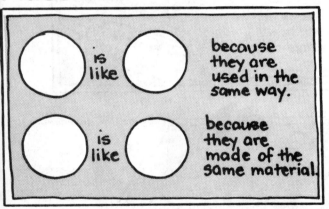

Placemat

Beginning Sounds

A set of task cards is made to go with the
beginning sounds being studied.
Children build with the things they find.
The task card may suggest a direction or
pattern for building.

Find junk that begins with the
1
2
3

Make something with the junk.

Find junk that
begins with these
letters.

s
t
b
m m

Make something
like this.

Find things
that begin with S.

Build something
with them.

Find things that
begin with these
letters.

p
f
t
b

Build up

Start with a large drawing or real object. Children add or hook on objects found in a junk box or center or in a dress-up corner that begin with the same sound. For example, for B, start with a drawing of a bear. Children could add on buttons, bracelet, bonnet, basket, balloon, box, bolt, band-aid, etc.

ABC Junk List
(Containers for products showing brand names can also be used—Jell-o box)

A —acorns, animal crackers
B —beans, beads, buttons, bolts, boxes, band-aid boxes
C —caps, cartons, cards, cans, cardboard, cotton, corks
D —dolls, dice, dinosaurs (plastic), decals
E —eggshells, earrings
F —funnels, felt, fabric, frames, foil
G —gears, gloves, glue bottles, glitter
H —hangers, hinges
I —Indians (plastic), ink bottles
J —jewelry, jars, jacks, juice cans
K —keys
L —lids, locks, lightbulbs, lima beans
M —meat trays, matchbooks, marshmallows, macaroni
N —nails, nuts, newspaper
O —oats, oatmeal box
P —pie pans, paper plates, pipes, postcards, plastic, pine cones
Q —quill
R —rings, rubber toy, rocks, rope
S —screws, string, straws, screen, sand, sponges, soap, sparkplugs, seeds, styrofoam, springs
T —toothpicks, tubes, tins, toys, tires (toy)
U —utensil
V —valentines, vases, vacuum cleaner parts, veil, velvet
W—washers, wig box, wool, watercolor boxes
X —x-rays (ask your doctor)
Y —yarn, yardsticks, yogurt carton
Z —zippers

Make a set of cards, each listing several letters. Children choose a card, find junk that begins with the letters, and arrange the junk into a collage.

Placemat

Cover each license plate letter with a piece of junk that begins with the same sound.

BTC

Collections

Junk collections are made up of objects in the same general category. The materials are gathered and stored in one area for use with specific activities. In most instances, these activities were developed to match the inherent properties of the objects in the collection. For example, counting activities go well with jewelry, whereas experiments with volume relate better to containers.

List of Collections

- Wood
- Hardware—nuts and bolts, screws, nails, hinges, etc.
- Discarded appliances and machinery
- Tools and utensils
- Boxes
- Clothing
- Toys
- Paper
- Plastic
- Parts—odds and ends left over from games, toys, household items
- Badge or label
- Source collection—discards from one particular source such as a supermarket, factory
- Comic books
- Magazines

Jewelry

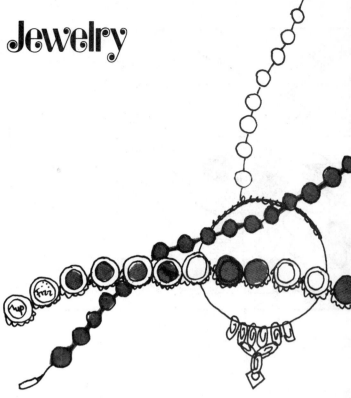

Duplicate the pattern of a piece of jewelry using macaroni, brads, rubber bands, washers, tags, bottle caps, wire, string, or paper clips. Use the same materials to create an original piece of jewelry.

Make a set of jewelry looking for pieces having like qualities. Describe the set in words or pictures.

Put on jewelry according to jewelry dress-up cards. Directions on these cards should include parts of the body, right or left, and the material of the jewelry.

Some ideas for storage and display . . .

- Manzanita branch
- Jewelry box
- Plastic chest

- Jewelry bulletin board

Write or dictate a story about a person wearing a piece of jewelry which is selected randomly from a grab bag.

Write descriptive words on tags and hook them onto a piece of jewelry.

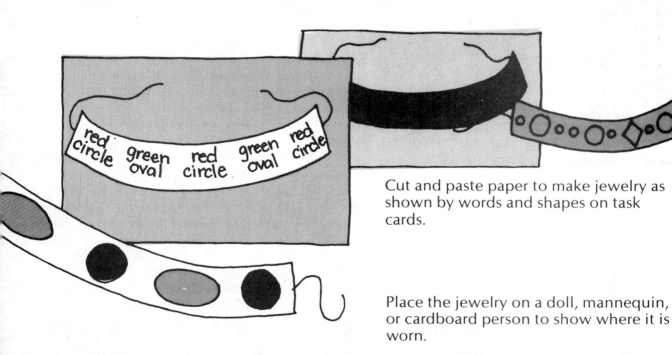

Cut and paste paper to make jewelry as shown by words and shapes on task cards.

Place the jewelry on a doll, mannequin, or cardboard person to show where it is worn.

Match the jewelry to the task card according to the number of pieces it has.

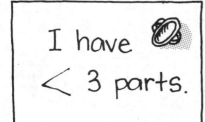

I have < 3 parts.

I have 4 parts.

I have > 7 parts.

FABRICS

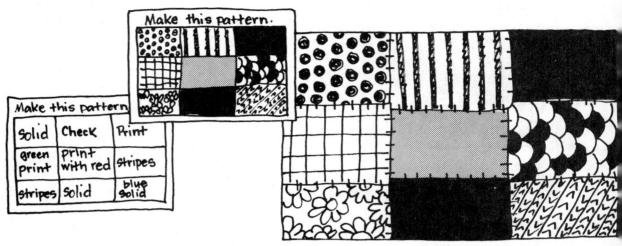

Make this pattern.

Solid	Check	Print
green print	print with red	stripes
stripes	Solid	blue solid

Make a picture collection by cutting and pasting from newspapers and magazines to show the different ways fabrics are used for clothing, furniture, and household items.

Sort fabrics according to their designs such as polka dots, stripes, prints, and plaids.

Sew, glue, or staple a patchwork design to match a pattern shown in pictures, fabrics, or words on a task card.

Extend the design of a fabric swatch by continuing the pattern onto a piece of paper using any media. Fabric may be selected by children or it can be prepasted to half of a sheet of paper.

Match two pieces of the same fabric to continue the design.

Estimate the number of one-inch stripes it would take to fill up different-sized surfaces. Then prove it by laying on the stripes and counting. This activity may also be done with polka dots, checks, and other patterns in varying dimensions.

Change a color in a swatch of fabric by making it lighter, darker, hotter, cooler, or in complimentary colors according to the directions on a chart or cards. Show the change on paper using crayons, paint, or chalk.

Place fabric, buttons, zippers, lace, and bows on a dress, pants, shirt, or blouse cut out of construction paper or cardboard.

Create a pattern on old white sheets or solid colored cloth as directed by a task card. The pattern can be made by placing the real objects on the cloth or by drawing them.

NATURE

Match riddle cards to nature objects which solve the riddle. Some riddle cards might read, "I am a home" (nest or shell) or "I have veins, and I am green" (a leaf).

Nature Collectibles

- thorns
- buds
- seeds
- petals
- shells
- weeds
- feathers
- twigs
- bark
- insects
- stems
- soil
- fur
- skins
- bones
- pods
- cones
- fronds

Experiment with nature objects to see which ones sink and which float.

Scratch objects with a nail to find out what is inside. Sort the objects into sets according to what is discovered.

Glue an object from nature on a piece of paper. Add drawings to complete a picture. For example, a bird could be drawn to complete a picture using a feather.

Match nature objects to rhyming word cards. A shell could be matched to a card with the word bell.

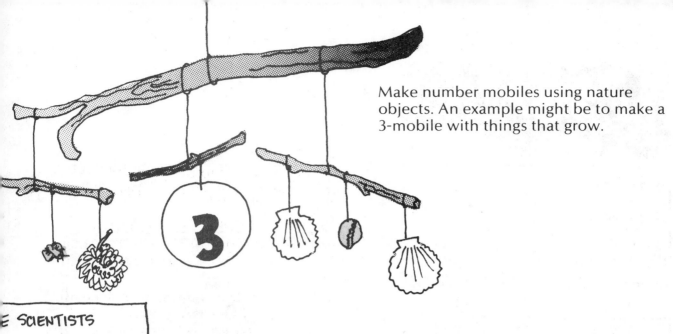

Make number mobiles using nature objects. An example might be to make a 3-mobile with things that grow.

Set up a bug box using an old aquarium or screened enclosure. Make an observation chart or tape observations of what happens in the box.

Design a method for displaying a personal collection of nature objects.

Make nature color wheels using real objects to show shades within a color. Sections may be labeled to name the various hues such as sandy brown, earth brown, spring leaf green, etc.

Create an environment in a box using objects from nature. Environments might be of mountain, seashore, underground, or jungle types.

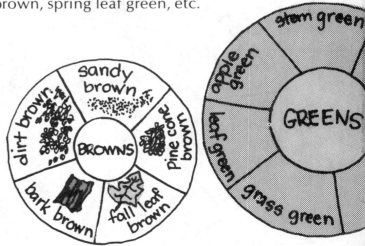

Food

Food Notes

Don't forget to do tasting and cooking with the collection.
Try making soups . . . great for leftover odds and ends.

Arrange food in order from sweet to sour, large to small, dark to light.

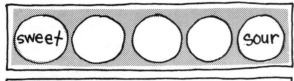

Experiment with seeds, bulbs, tubers, and parts of other foods to see which will grow.

Match food objects or words to each section of a large color wheel.

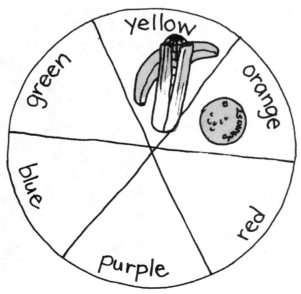

Eat a piece of food. Find the mouth with the word that tells how you ate it and place the word on the flannel board face.

Serve a TV dinner that matches food items to beginning or ending sounds written on the serving tray.

Estimate and prove by counting the following things about food: the number of seeds, sections, or leaves that it has; the number of twists needed to pull off the stem.

Fill and weigh different sized bags labeled with the same amount, such as one pound. Explain why some bags have more pieces of food and why some are more filled than others.

Food Notes

Foods that last:
- artichokes
- potatoes
- onions
- nuts in shells
- squash
- citrus fruits
- marshmallows
- hard candies
- dry cereals
- licorice

Introduce exotic foods into the collection from time to time:
- lichee nuts
- jicama
- ginger root
- mango
- seaweed

Use artificial foods for those that are hard to find or perish easily:
- plastic
- papier-mâché
- toys
- straw

Experiment with foods to find out which can be used as dyes.

Rub the inside and outside of food on paper to see which part of the food will produce a smell.

Place the word, picture, or actual piece of food on the placemat to complete the phrase.

Listen to a tape recording of sounds of food being eaten to guess what food it is.

Look at and memorize food arranged on a tray while a friend counts to ten. Select food from a box to duplicate the arrangement. Compare the second tray with the first one.

Pack a sack lunch by following the directions on the bag which indicate the quantity of food to be packed and the source of the food.

Projects

A junk project is something that a child creates from the materials available to him. The beginning point for a junk project can be the child's natural inclination to build or an experience he has had. The teacher can initiate junk projects by providing opportunities through field trips, books, films, or discussions which arouse the child's interest to build and by making materials for building available. By watching children and listening to them as they work and play, the teacher can determine when a child is ready for a junk project and what direction the project might take.

Although the building process is a learning experience in itself, it can be enhanced by the teacher's ability to suggest activities relating to the object the child has constructed. Discovery, experimentation, and research should be the basis of these activities. The learning possibilities are dictated by the child's interest level and the quality of the teacher's intervention.

The use of Building Starter Cards widens the alternatives for building projects. These cards can stimulate a child to select a junk project, or they can be used as a follow-up activity after a child has completed a project. Building Starter Cards also expand the creative process by indicating the varied ways a piece of junk can be used. The clues for how to complete a project reinforce the acquisition of problem solving skills. The format of these cards emphasizes both developing and practicing basic skills such as sorting, matching, and classifying.

The following junk project pages have four parts:

1. Children's play activity or product as starting point for project work
2. Suggested materials for building
3. Examples of projects children have constructed
4. Ideas for activities that extend learnings from the project. These can also be used as:
   - starter questions to initiate a project
   - task cards or charts for independent projects
   - intervention questions when working or conferencing with a child
   - related topics for any project

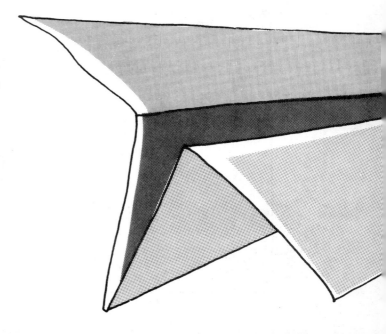

AIRPLANES

Extending Learnings After Building . . .

Fly the airplane indoors and outdoors to discover how far it will go. Graph or measure the discovery.

Experiment by adding or taking away something from the airplane to discover what will happen to how it looks or moves.

Draw and categorize the shapes that were used for the airplane's parts.

Use reference books and pictures to label the airplane's parts.

Experiment with different weights, kinds, and sizes of paper to make an airplane. Discover how flying is affected by each.

Try folding paper in different ways to make an airplane. Duplicate or diagram one of these airplane models.

Fly airplanes upside down and from different heights. Draw what happens.

Make a tape recording of noises that airplanes make.

Suggested Materials

- meat trays
- wood scraps
- cardboard tubes
- egg cartons
- boxes
- marshmallows, licorice
- buttons
- saran wrap, cellophane

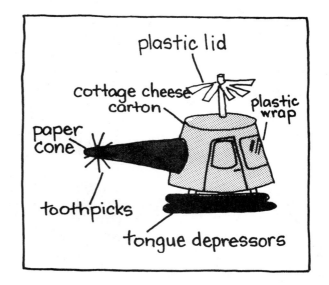

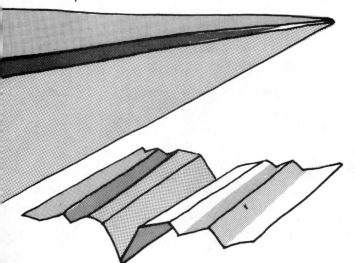

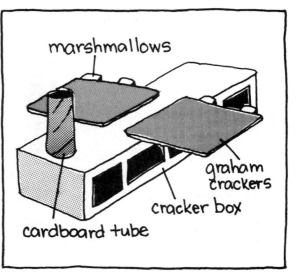

Extending Learnings
After Building . . .

Stack objects to build a tower on a circular and a square base to discover which will hold the highest tower.

Place the heaviest piece of junk for the tower on the bottom, middle, and top to discover what happens when it is in each position.

Compare the measurements of students' towers to discover which is the highest, widest, longest, and shortest.

Replicate a famous tower.

Build a word tower with tower words, such as TALL, HIGH, LOFTY, and SOARING.

Make a "tower of power" using cartoon words, such as ZAP, BOOM, KA-ZAM, etc.

Suggested Materials
- straws
- styrofoam packing stuff
- cardboard tubes
- playing cards
- paper plates and cups
- scraps of wood

Boats

Suggested Materials

- styrofoam
- straws, ice cream sticks
- fabric
- sponges
- toothpicks
- paper plates
- record disks
- wood scraps

Extending Learnings
After Building . . .

Experiment to see if the boat will float.

Design a code using flags for the boat.

Write or dictate a log of the boat's voyage.

Name the boat and create an insignia for it.

Draw a picture of yourself as the captain of the boat.

Find out the different ways boats move, such as with oars, sails, paddles, and engines. Build a boat that moves by one of these methods.

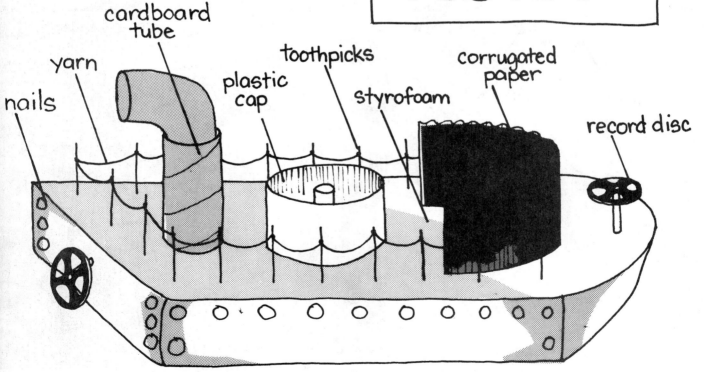

SPACE VEHICLES

Suggested Materials

- paper plates and cups
- string, yarn
- balloons
- plastic bags
- paper clips, brads
- cans
- tin foil, saran wrap
- nails, wire

Extending Learnings
After Building . . .

Design a station or site for the space vehicle to use in taking off or landing.

Paint the space vehicle to match the flag of a country.

Dictate a news bulletin to report a happening about the space vehicle.

Illustrate what happens first, second, and third while the space vehicle is in operation.

Make an astronaut uniform to wear.

Duplicate actual star patterns or create new ones.

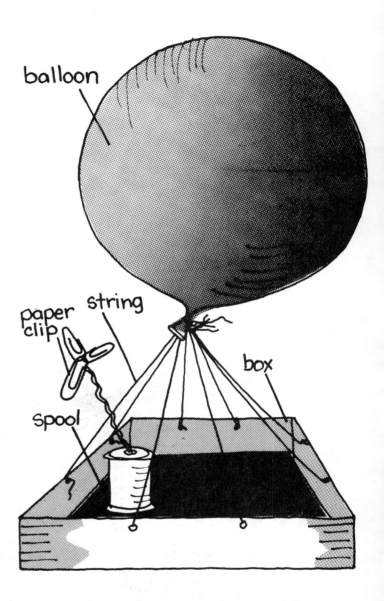

Cars

Suggested Materials

- cardboard tubes
- boxes, trays
- wood scraps
- buttons
- bottle tops, lids
- marshmallows
- saran wrap, cellophane

Extending Learnings
After Building . . .

Change the style of the car by designing and adding new parts, such as headlights, fenders, and bumpers.

Experiment to see how the car runs on different types of surfaces, such as lawn, sand, and pavement.

Make a collection of vehicles with wheels using models or pictures.

Experiment with different ways to make the car move, such as balloons, string, magnets, batteries, and pinwheels.

Take a survey of teachers and parents to find out the types of mechanical difficulties that affect cars most often.

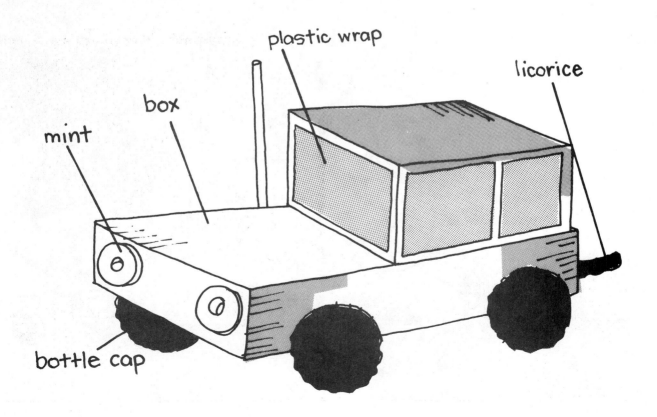

HOUSES

Suggested Materials

- wood scraps
- carpet, wallpaper, linoleum, fabric samples
- boxes, cartons
- ice cream sticks
- sugar cubes, graham crackers
- sponges
- plastic trays, dividers

Extending Learnings
After Building . . .

Experiment with real or simulated weather conditions to find out the effects on the house.

Create a real estate listing for the house telling size, location, description, and price.

Design a floor plan for the house.

Redesign the house into an apartment, mobile home, or part of a community complex.

Make furniture for the house.

Make houses for storybook characters, such as the Three Little Pigs, the Three Bears, and Snow White and the Seven Dwarfs.

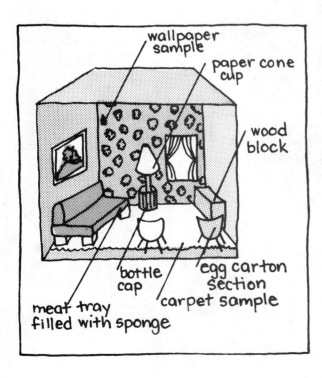

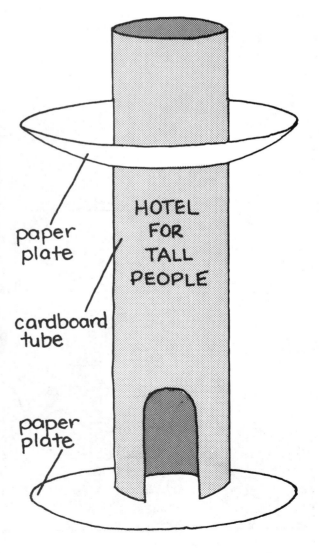

Robots

Suggested Materials

- frozen juice cans
- springs
- nuts and bolts
- cardboard tubes
- tin foil, foil trays
- light bulbs
- parts of appliances, watches
- transistor batteries
- straws, string
- paper cups and plates
- old silverware

Extending Learnings
After Building . . .

Design a control panel to "operate" the robot.

Write a Help-Wanted Ad for the robot describing jobs for it to do.

Diagram the inside workings of the robot.

Find similarities and differences between the robot and the student who made it, comparing such characteristics as height, weight, color, age, and shape.

Survey classmates to find out what information they would like to know about the robot. Make a tape which could be played from behind the robot to give this information.

Make the robot into a "Fact Man" by creating a tape that teaches a specific subject or skill to other students.

Design or make clothes for the robot for various jobs and occasions.

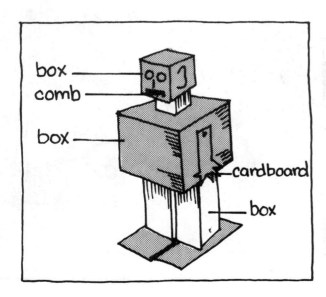

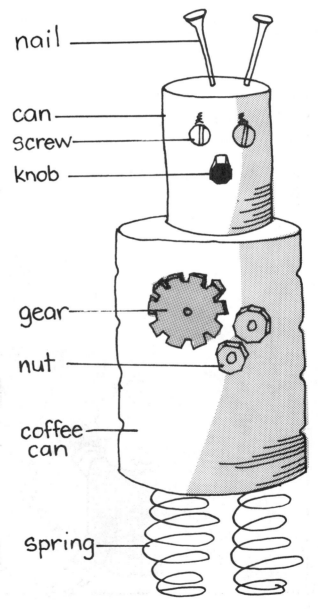

People

Suggested Materials

- plastic bottles
- cups, paper plates
- yarn, fabric
- clothespins
- fruit baskets
- pipe cleaners
- paper bags
- egg cartons, milk cartons

Extending Learnings
After Building . . .

Add appropriate accessories to change the person into a storybook character, such as Cinderella, Porky Pig, or Pinocchio.

Make a twin or a friend for the person.

Design faces for the person to show such emotions as happy, angry, sad, or fearful.

Reconstruct the person to make him taller, shorter, fatter, or thinner.

Write a birth certificate for the person telling birthdate, weight, height, birthplace, and parents.

Make ethnic people dolls.

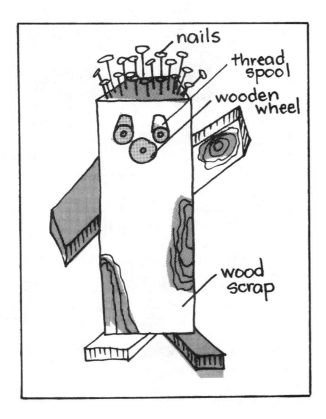

nails

thread spool

wooden wheel

wood scrap

yarn

paper cup

pipe cleaner

fabric

tube

Building Starter Cards

FIND AND FINISH

Find these.

Put them together.

Finish it to make something to live in.

FIND AND FINISH

Find these.

Put them together.

Finish it to make something that moves.

COPY AND FINISH

Copy this.

Finish it to make something for an astronaut.

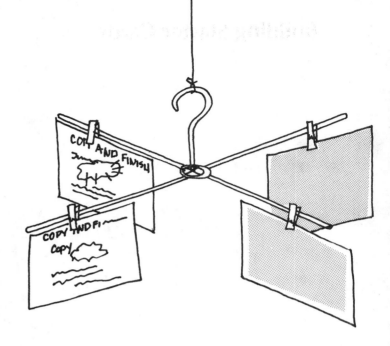

COPY AND FINISH

Copy this.

Finish it to make
a crazy animal.

COPY AND FINISH

Copy this.

Finish it. What will
you make?

Choose 4 things you
can eat.

Choose 3 containers
that once held food.

Build a food store.

Use it to play store.

MORE

Choose silver junk:
2 shiny ones
2 dull ones
4 round ones
3 square ones
Build a silver sculpture.
Put it on display in the office.

Choose 6 paper things.
Choose 5 metal things.
Choose 1 plastic thing.
Build something that hangs.
Hang it in the room.

Find the

egg carton   marshmallow

Put them together.

make a

Choose an equal number of two different kinds of junk.
Build anything
Describe it to the teacher.

4=4
3=3
6=6

Choose 10 thir
Some of these mus
be round.
Some of these must be straight.
Build something that carri
things.
Draw a picture of it.

Choose 2 objects from nature.
Choose 2 man-made objects.
Build something that an animal can use.
Tell a friend how it can be used.

Oldies But Goodies

Blocks, playhouse equipment, and other apparatus have traditionally been an integral part of early childhood education. An innovative learning program is not one that casts aside these materials, but one that retains them and the ways they have been used while providing opportunities for new and different uses.

The following pages show materials that have long been standard classroom equipment and yet are still relevant to the needs and interests of children. The activities have been designed to extend the materials' uses into broader and perhaps different areas. In some instances the activities help teach a skill; in others they provide extension experiences for older or more able students. The activities are meant to show that new ideas and new settings can be organized around traditional but still valuable materials.

BLOCKS

The teacher makes several sets of cards which name different parts of a given setting and places them in envelopes. Children may use the titles on the envelopes as a suggestion for building. The labels in the envelopes can also give children suggestions of buildings to place within a given setting. The children can use the cards after building to label their constructions.

The teacher provides several floor mats made of vinyl, oilcloth, or paper. Block shapes are outlined on each floor mat. A child chooses a floor mat and lays on the matching blocks.

The teacher cuts several sizes of squares out of vinyl or oilcloth. A child chooses a square, covers the entire surface with blocks, and counts the number of blocks he used. Children can also compare how many blocks are used in covering the different sizes of squares or in covering the same square with different sized blocks.

Children lay out a maze. Mazes can be used by animals, toy cars, or other children.

Collect wood scraps. Have children saw, sand, paint, and varnish the wood to make a new set of classroom blocks. Each child can design and sign his block.

SAND

A collection of many granular substances is set up for children to experiment with by feel. Some substances to include are oats, sugar, corn meal, salt, rice, dry cereal, flour, and cornstarch. A child compares each substance to the feeling of sand. He can describe comparisons of texture or consistency orally or by using prepared cards or worksheets on which he glues his selection.

A collection of sets of containers for quarts, pints, liters, and gallons is made by the teacher and students. One set is used to build molded sand cities.

A child chooses several objects to imprint into wet sand. Other children guess what object made the imprint and check their response by finding the object and trying to make a matching print.

The teacher or a child buries an object in the sand. Treasure Hunt directions are made up for another child to use in locating the treasure. Directions can include words such as north, south, west, and east, and left and right, and distances to measure with a ruler or other measuring device.

Playhouse

A child chooses one or more household chores from a chart hanging in the playhouse. He sets a timer for 5, 10, or 15 minutes and tries to beat the clock in completing the chores. Older children might graph or chart their times in doing various chores.

Using a phone book they have made of numbers important to them, children look up a number, try to remember it, and dial it on a play telephone.

Children fill in a weekly calendar listing the chores to be done each day.

Using a paper plate, saucer, cup, and napkin, a child designs a place setting to be used in the playhouse. The basic design will be repeated in whole or in part on the different pieces of the setting.

Make several tablecloths with printed instructions. Children place objects on the tablecloth according to directions.

Put a plate in the middle.

Put a pan on your left.
Put a plate on your right.
Put a cup above the pan.

Play Equipment

Set up signs and chalk paths leading to various locations such as the moon, the seashore, the mountains, and the desert. A child chooses a place to visit and packs a suitcase with items selected from a collection in a box. He can also make the items needed for his visit. He then selects a piece of play equipment and follows the path to his destination.

Make a simple floor map and matching ditto showing houses and streets. Label boxes or bags with addresses or colors of houses and fill with objects to be delivered. A child chooses an object, plots his route on the ditto, and with a piece of play equipment, follows the route on the floor map to make the delivery.

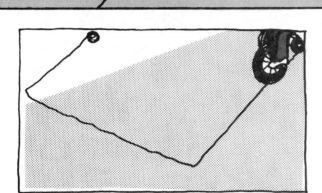

Cut a long length of string and lay it on the playground in a straight line. Time a child as he rides along the string on a piece of play equipment. Rearrange the string into other configurations, such as a circle, square, or squiggle, and compare the time it takes to travel along each one. Discussions should be held as to why some shapes take longer than others to travel. Older children can extend what they have learned to estimating differences in time needed to travel on roads shown on maps. For example, they could experiment with rulers and toy cars and discuss the difference between a straight road and a winding, mountain road.

Choose a theme for a parade from among holidays, comic strips, TV programs, book characters, circus or zoo animals, sports heroes, or astronauts. Children decorate the play equipment to represent a float for the parade.

3.
ME
EXPERIENCES

	Agree	Uncertain	Disagree
• *A child attends school to learn subjects and skills.*			
• *A child attends school to learn about himself.*			
• *A child attends school to learn about other people.*			
• *A child attends school to learn about his cultural or ethnic group.*			

A teacher's attitude toward affective learning can be shown by the responses made to these statements.

All of a child's experiences lead to the development and assessment of who he is. The affective growth of a child should be interwoven with his cognitive growth. A child's understanding of who he is, is aided by his finding out what he knows, what he can do, and how others see him. These are interdependent learnings.

The activities in this section have been developed to help increase a child's awareness of himself as an individual. Simultaneously, the activities encourage the child to expand his knowledge and skills in various subject areas. Because the outcomes of affective learnings are personally related to the child, the teacher must set the stage for the experience rather than teach to the experience. The child's responses to an affective experience cannot be evaluated as either right or wrong. The worth of the experience should be assessed in terms of the progress a child makes in being better able to perceive himself and others.

This chapter has been structured in the same order as the child experiences the world. Activities that focus on the child as the center of his world are followed by those dealing with the child and his interaction with others. Some possible results of a child's participation in Me experiences include:

- Awareness of the physical self
- Identification of learned tasks and personal accomplishments
- Clarification of values
- Empathy and cooperation in personal relationships
- Appreciation of likenesses and differences among people
- Cultural awareness

As the teacher plans for and evaluates affective experiences, she must keep in mind that the process of answering the question Who Am I? is a lifelong one. The teacher needs to recognize the importance of this process and to ensure that there is a place for it in the classroom curriculum. The teacher needs to be aware and take advantage of every informal or structured learning experience to further the child's affective development.

This Is Me

Children make their own Yea and Boo banners. Likes are written on the Yea banner and dislikes on the Boo banner. Banners can be displayed in the room to stimulate further discussion.

Provide each child with a large sheet of paper for a Me collage. As Me activities, such as weighing, measuring, identifying eye, hair, and skin color and other physical attributes, are completed, children add representations of their findings to their Me collages. A collection of materials such as lengths of string, magazine pictures of people, colored chalk, paints and pens, and fabric swatches can be provided.

Children make numerology charts describing themselves. A chart would include all the pertinent numbers of a child's life such as his birthdate, weight, height, address, phone number, and number of family members.

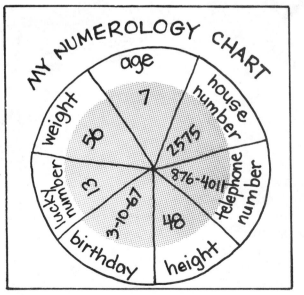

Children use the crystal ball to tell what they will be like in the future: their appearances, their jobs, their hobbies, their family lives. They should give reasons for their predictions. Children can learn the language of a fortune teller, pretending to be one as they tell their own fortunes to others.

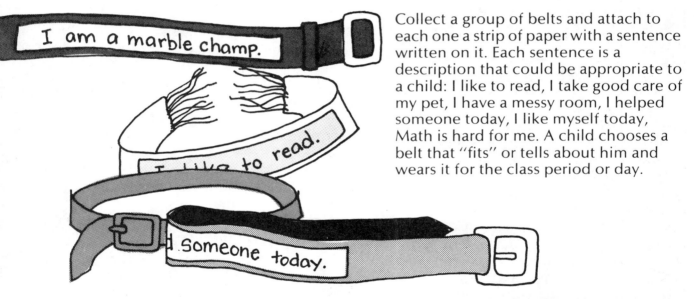

Collect a group of belts and attach to each one a strip of paper with a sentence written on it. Each sentence is a description that could be appropriate to a child: I like to read, I take good care of my pet, I have a messy room, I helped someone today, I like myself today, Math is hard for me. A child chooses a belt that "fits" or tells about him and wears it for the class period or day.

A student makes an exhibit about himself to place in the Exhibition Hall. It may be made of objects, photos, or pictures. The student may exhibit things that tell about his life since babyhood, his interests, his pets, or his favorite things.

One child acts as a quick-sketch artist and makes a drawing of a student passer-by. A maximum time, such as three minutes, can be set, and a timer can be used to keep track of the time. The artist tries to find the unique qualities of the person he sketches.

Children fill a purse, pocket, or parcel with objects that are important to them such as favorite possessions, often worn clothes, or something showing a hobby or special interest. By figuring out which child a set of objects might be important to, other children can guess who filled the purse, pocket, or parcel.

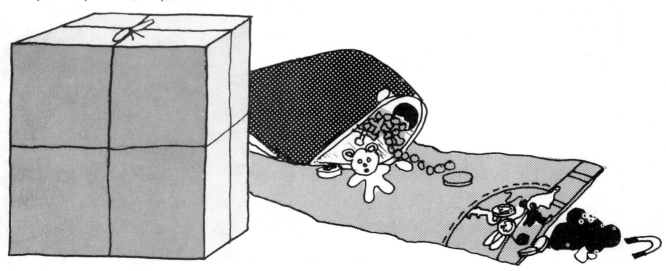

Me and My Feelings

Faces are cut from magazines. These are pasted onto paper and divided in half to form two parts of a book. The third part contains various written situations. Children choose a situation page and find the upper and lower portions of faces that best express the emotion they would feel in that situation.

All of these activities will be more meaningful to the children if time is arranged for small and large group discussions. Remember, there are no right or wrong answers.

Possibilities for Situation Cards

- My friend just pushed me down.
- Everybody else wants to go to the zoo.
- Somebody called me a bad name.
- The teacher didn't choose me.
- My money is gone.
- He's copying me.
- Someone tore my paper.
- She made me cry.
- My teacher said, "That's great!"
- My little brother/sister got a new toy and I didn't.
- I broke my mom's best dish.
- Our pet died.
- I won first place.
- Nobody likes me.
- I got to do it first.

Label envelopes with names of emotions, such as anger, fear, sadness, pride, and happiness. Fill envelopes with lengths of colored yarn, one color for each emotion, for example, yellow for sadness and red for anger. Make a set of situation cards. A child chooses a situation card, writes his name on it, and ties into it different colors of yarn to correspond with the feelings he would have in that circumstance.

Write names of emotions on a spinner. Children spin to a word and show all the ways they can portray the emotion. They can act out situations, and use body movements, voice, and facial expressions. A mirror can help the child see himself as he portrays the emotion.

A problem or situation is chosen that has occurred or may occur with the class. Alternative plans of action and the consequences of each action are discussed and recorded. Each child can decide which alternative he would choose.

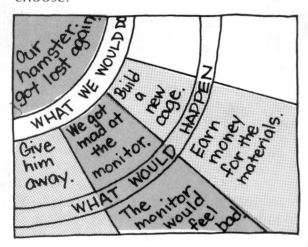

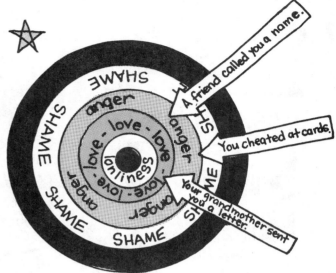

Write situations children might experience on paper arrows. A child places an arrow on the target pointing to the emotion he would feel in the situation described on his arrow. The whole class may use one large target or individual targets may be made for each child.

A child makes a photo album of himself showing his many emotions through pictures. The photos may be old or recent ones, or the child can have a friend take some candids in the classroom. The photos may be labeled and the emotion explained.

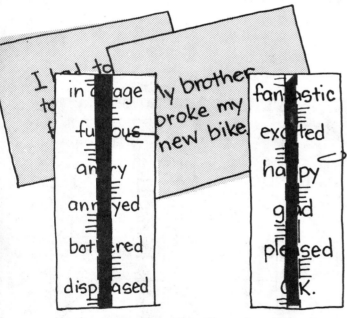

Make thermometers showing the ranges of several emotions. Children select a situation card and move a clip on the thermometer to show what degree of the emotion they would feel in that situation.

I Can Do It Myself

Each child makes his own big letter I out of butcher paper and shows by words, drawings, or cut-out pictures all the things he can do by himself.

Write "I wish I could———" on coin-shaped papers and place them near a model of a wishing well. A child writes a wish on a coin and drops it into the well. Periodically coins may be taken from the well, and other children may volunteer to help make someone's wish come true. The teacher might use the coins to help her plan for skill or activity groups.

Use large boxes, bookcases, or tables as booths for a Country Fair. Children exhibit their own handicrafts, foods, and other materials made at home or school. Plans and schedules can be made for children interested in demonstrating or teaching their craft to others.

Set up several "clotheslines." Each line shows related tasks from a simple to a difficult level. As children successfully perform a task, they move a clothespin showing their name to that place on the line.

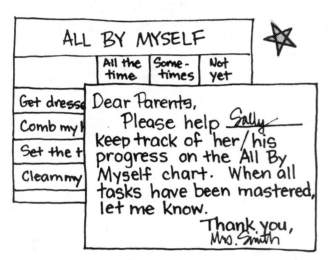

Using a prepared form, children and parents discuss the tasks a child can do at home. Jointly they keep an ongoing record of the tasks on this form. This activity encourages parents to become involved with the growth of their children. A cover letter may be included to explain the form to parents.

Make a set of cards with pictures of objects that represent tasks children do such as tying a shoe and zipping a zipper. Children select a card and use real objects to perform the task pictured on the card. They then sort the cards into the three categories:
    By Myself
    With Help
    Not Yet

Me and Other People

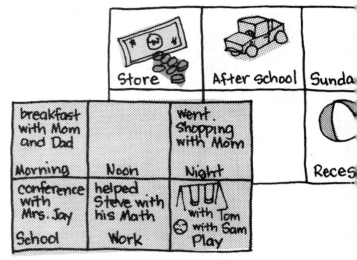

An International Marketplace is set up on a table top and bookshelves or on an available floor space. Booths are built or outlined on large paper or vinyl and labeled. Displays for each country are made of real objects, or pictures of products may be drawn or cut out of magazines and newspapers. International foods and cooking could be incorporated by having a tasting party at the end of each day or week.

Major categories such as times of the day and places or activities are outlined on a worksheet or placemat. Children indicate in words, pictures, or real objects the actions they would enter into with other people in each of the categories.

Specific tasks are outlined in words or pictures on a chart. Children perform each task alone and then repeat the task working cooperatively with another child or a small group of children. They compare the two performances of the task by recording such things as their feelings, ease of accomplishment, problems that occurred, and quality of the end results.

Index cards are prepared with a different country's name written in each stamp corner. A child selects a card, finds out about how people live in the country named on the card, and draws the people of the country on the reverse side of the card. When several of these "postcards" are finished, children might start a class post office and "mail" them to each other, using travel messages, foreign words, and appropriate addresses.

Children choose the medallion of a country and become the ambassador for that country. Then they design and construct an art piece or a model of a famous landmark of their country to present as a gift to the U.S. ambassador.

In a listening booth a child chooses one selection from a group of records or tapes of different ethnic pieces. While listening to the music, he accompanies it by playing appropriate or matching instruments which he has chosen from a collection kept at the booth. Families can be involved by sending in various pieces of music and kinds of instruments.

On large sheets of paper make life-size drawings of one-half of a child's form. Children choose one of these drawings and match it to themselves, comparing their own shapes, parts, and size to the drawing.

Set up a chart rack or clothesline and hangers as an Around the World Fashion Shop. Children design and construct ethnic costumes using cloth or paper. Children might also collect or bring from home examples of ethnic clothing. Another variation would be for children to sort pictures of articles of clothing by hanging them in different ethnic sections of the fashion shop.

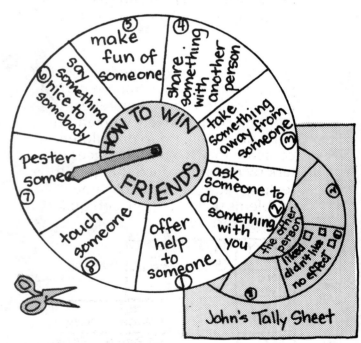

To play "How to Win Friends," a child spins the spinner and performs the indicated task. Then he records on his worksheet the effect of his action on the other person involved. After several turns, responses on worksheets are tallied and discussions are held regarding the effects of one's actions on others.

Me and Other Creatures

Children create and add to an "Animal Believe It or Not" book, comic strip, chart, or bulletin board. Strange or interesting facts can be gathered from books, films, tapes, observation, and interviews with veterinarians, zoo workers, and pet shop personnel.

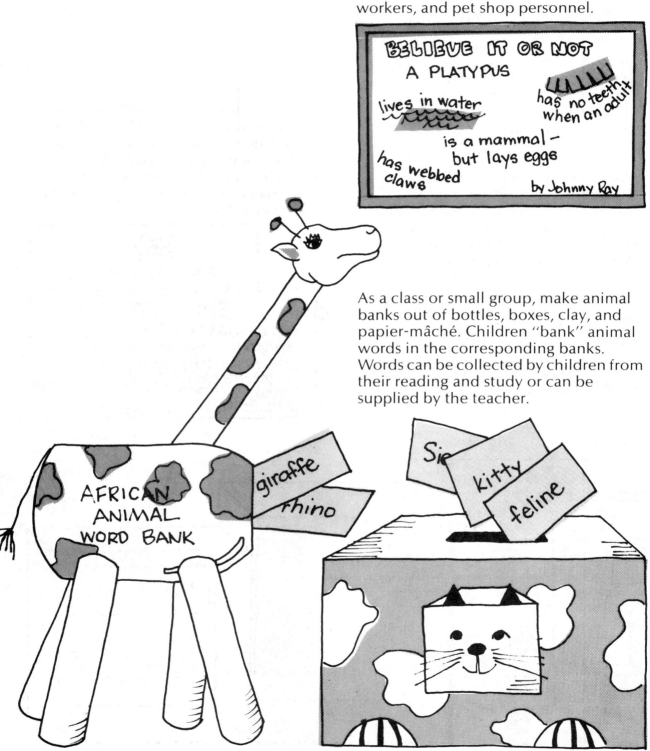

As a class or small group, make animal banks out of bottles, boxes, clay, and papier-mâché. Children "bank" animal words in the corresponding banks. Words can be collected by children from their reading and study or can be supplied by the teacher.

Children name animals based on the type of animal or where it came from. For example, a German shepherd might be named Heidi or Schnitzel, a kangaroo, Matilda or Canberra.

Make a collection of photographs or drawings of animal homes such as warrens, dens, and nests. From a supply of natural material housed in the classroom or collected by the class, children construct and label a replica of an animal home.

Children make a Pet Care Store out of boxes or a bookcase. The store is stocked with real foods, pet care items, empty food containers, or drawings and pictures cut out of magazines. Labels, store decorations, and advertisements, as well as charts or booklets on animal care, are added to the store.

Children earn Veterinarian Diplomas by finding and sharing knowledge about the needs, care, and training of favorite animals. Some additional resources to consider: animal shelter, local veterinarian, community expert, and pet store personnel.

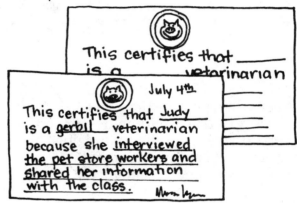

Set up a laboratory with animals such as mice, hamsters, ants or other insects, and fish. From questions raised by observations in the lab, children design experiments and keep records of hypotheses, procedures, and results. Experiments might be based on observing and comparing eating patterns, training, social habits, and behavior of different animals.

A child chooses an animal or species that needs protection. Based on his knowledge or study of the animal's habitat, he constructs a model of a game preserve. Signs, posters, or a handbook of rules can be made for the preserve.

Organize a classroom or school Pet Week when pets are brought to visit for a morning or day. Children design and prepare prizes, criteria for judging, categories of animals for each day, and pens or equipment needed.

Animal Group Words
- farrow—pigs
- swarm—bees
- colony—ants
- flock—sheep
- pack—wolves
- school—fish
- herd—cattle
- covey—partridge
- bevy—quail

Make an animal game using a spinner, dice, and group names. Children, in turn, roll the dice, name the animals indicated by the group name on the spinner, and, if correct, mark a tally sheet with the number shown on the dice. At the end of the game, the child with the highest number of animals wins. The game can be varied by accumulating plastic or paper animals or animal decals instead of marking on a tally sheet.

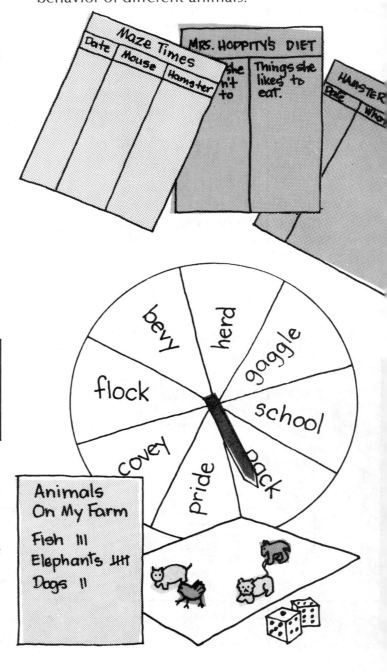

Children gather information about endangered species and rare animals. Then they choose an animal and set up a "Save the Animal" campaign by making brochures, posters, and slogans, and by writing letters to concerned people or groups.

Children design a zoo for famous animals they have learned about or know from movies, TV, history, sports, and literature. The zoo can have genus and species names, information posters, and maps showing where the animals are found in the world.

Me and My Decisions

Design a ballot box and set up a mini-chalkboard or small section of the board with a title such as "Issues of the Day." List one or two issues that come up during the day. After some discussion on pros and cons, children vote. The vote is tallied and posted until new issues arise and new votes are taken. A permanent booklet of issues and voting outcomes can be kept throughout the year as a record of the class's problems and solutions.

Collect a number of shoe boxes or other containers. Put an object in each box which represents a classroom situation, such as a note to be delivered or a ball to be given out for recess. The teacher or the child takes one box and gives the object to an individual or group for their use. The class members decide if the choice was fair or unfair and give their reasons for their choice. Their decision is tallied and recorded. The activity can be repeated at various times to see if the class decision changes.

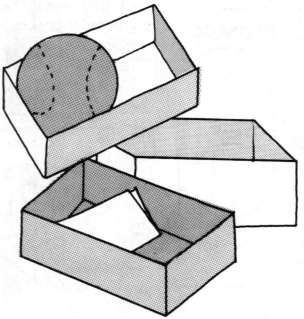

Make an "If the Shoe Fits, Wear It" shoe bag. Label the pockets. Write decision statements on paper shoe shapes. Children take turns filling the pockets with shoes that correspond to who makes decisions in their own lives.

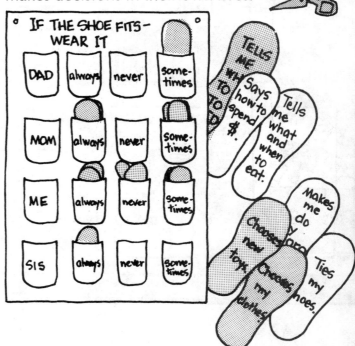

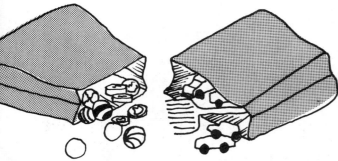

Fill two bags with the same number but different kinds of toys and other objects valued by children. Two children are selected and are each given one of the bags. After they examine the contents of both bags, they bargain and trade items with each other. Other children observe the exchange and interpret why the exchange worked out as it did.

Cut doors into a piece of heavy paper to make a building. Label the doors with descriptive words or phrases such as IS POLITE, MINDS, or SHARES WITH OTHERS. Label figures with an action such as SENT A CARD, PULLED PIGTAILS, or WALKED AWAY FROM GAME. A child takes a figure and places it behind the door that characterizes the action.

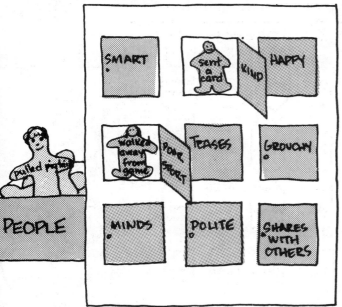

You are not allowed to go to the movies this week.

What made this happen?

...are getting ...n-speed bike ...present.

What made this happen?

On cards write or illustrate decisions children might make. Children draw a card and tell what they think happened to cause the decision to be made. They can also tell what they would need to do to have the decision changed.

Make a set of decision-making placemats. Children use pictures of situations or objects, or real things in filling the placemats.

4.
TALKING
EXPERIENCES

"It's that thing over there."
*"What do you mean? That fluffy
pink toy on the table?"*

This simple dialogue between two
children illustrates different levels of
language and suggests the need for
providing a classroom climate and a
selection of activities that aid in
developing verbal communication skills.
Formal and informal talking experiences
provide many opportunities for children
to engage in purposeful
communication.

Talking experiences capitalize on a
young child's natural enjoyment in
talking and motivate him to become
involved in speaking with others. As
children participate in the talking
experiences described in this section,
both incidental and more directed
communication occurs. The child's
words may describe his reactions to an
experience, or they may be a direct
response to the questions posed by an
activity. The acquisition of such
language skills as describing,
questioning, and responding is made
possible through experiences which
allow students to assume roles that
require unique vocabulary and language
styles. Through many of the activities
children learn and practice more precise
ways of speaking. In addition to
encouraging the development of
language skills and the socialization
process, these talking experiences
improve the quality of interchange
among children. Many of these activities
stimulate children to spontaneously
create their own talking experiences.

The measure of a child's need for and
success in a talking experience is made
through teacher observation. Listening
to students as they talk will assist the
teacher in diagnosing their needs and in
directing them to appropriate activities.
Children's informal talking is also a good
indicator of what they know and
understand about the world.

Some items for the teacher to observe
as children talk include:
- clarity of meaning
- fluency
- grammatical structure
- articulation patterns
- word and sound discrimination
- use of nonstandard cultural speech
  patterns or idioms

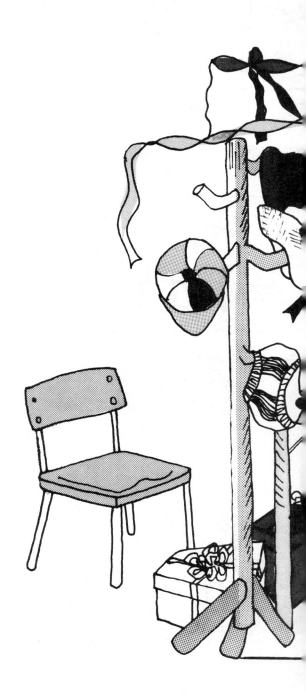

Happy Birthday Center

**. . . an example of activities
organized into a learning center**

Happy Birthday Center

Play a cooperation game of "Pin the ball on the seal's nose." Children play in pairs. The blindfolded child is given verbal directions by his partner, using words such as left, right, higher, lower.

Collect real hats or make paper hats for such people as a policeman, nurse, Santa Claus, and a construction worker. Children put on a hat and tell what the person would like for his birthday.

Make a birthday cake using cardboard or styrofoam. Make holes in it for candles. Children put candles in the holes, count them, and tell a birthday wish for each candle.

IT HAS NUMERALS AND A SHINY FACE. I'LL GIVE YOU ANOTHER CLUE - IT HAS HANDS.

I WISH EVERY DAY WERE MY BIRTHDAY. I WISH I HAD A NEW BIKE. I WISH UNCLE JOE WERE HERE. I WISH.....

Decorate boxes and place an object in each box. A child chooses a present, looks inside, and describes the present. Other children guess what is in the box.

Children use a play telephone to invite people to their party. They might invite their best friend, mother, teacher, or doctor. Children should be encouraged to include time, date, place, and directions to their home in the conversation.

Plan birthday parties for various animals, such as a kangaroo, an ant, or a monkey. Talk about what the presents could be, what food would be served, what games would be played, and who would be invited.

Set up two large charts with the titles Last Year's Birthday and My Next Birthday. Attach a pad of drawing paper to each chart. A child draws a scene on each pad, then tells about the scenes using past and future tenses.

Set up a box with a collection of pictures or objects. A child chooses something from the box and sings Happy Birthday to it. Rather than name the picture or object as he sings, he substitutes a description for the name. Other children try to guess what is being described in the song.

SALESMEN

... an example of related activities
placed in different locations around the
room

Collect various cosmetics and actor's makeup paint and store in an old suitcase or shopping bag. Children take turns being a cosmetic demonstrator and salesperson, either in door-to-door fashion or by setting up a demonstration table with mirror as in a department store. Color charts and other samples may be made, as well as drawings or diagrams of instructions for use of various items. Demonstration sessions can be scheduled by the salesperson with other students.

Salesmen

A child becomes a street vendor by designing and decorating a wagon, shopping cart, or a box on wheels as his peddler's cart. After listening to recordings or literature which include street vendor's cries, the child makes up his own yell for advertising his wares. Products may be made by the child or represented by drawings or models. Other children may participate as buyers, either from homes or businesses the vendor services.

Use the empty cabinet of an old TV or make a TV out of a large box. A child gets inside and performs a commercial he knows or makes up a new commercial for a product.

One child acts as a car salesman to several student prospective buyers. He makes up and delivers his sales pitch, giving information on special features, price, and mechanical points. Some props for the salesman to use include toy cars, drawings or photos of cars, and boxes and paper to represent a car lot.

Shoe boxes are labeled with size, price, and color. One child acts as a customer, describes the kind of shoes he needs, and tells where he will wear them. The salesman tries to find the shoes asked for or tries to convince the customer to buy another pair in stock.

Make a door out of cardboard or chart paper and hang on a chart rack. Put a container of products to be sold nearby. Each product is labeled with words describing it. For example, a candy box can be labeled with the words CHEWY, DELICIOUS, and PURE CHOCOLATE. One child acts as a door-to-door salesman, selling a product he has chosen. Another child is the customer behind the door.

Children make stadium vendors' boxes and fill them with wares to be sold. The items can be made by the children. The vendors peddle their wares by making up a descriptive jingle or slogan to attract buyers.

A gavel and a collection of objects become the props for an auction. After a discussion of the kind of language used by an auctioneer, one child chooses an object, describes it, and auctions it off. Other children act as bidders.

Speaker's Corner

Provide a box or any other podium for a soapbox speaker to use. Have children help draw up a list of unsettled problems or questions, such as: "Should Goldilocks have gone into the three bears' house?" "Should our school buy its own bus?" and "Should parents tell children what time to go to bed?" Each soapbox orator chooses a question and prepares and gives a talk to try to convince others of his viewpoint.

Ideas for Phone Booth Cards
- Your hair is too long.
- You need Chinese vegetables for dinner.
- Your bicycle has a flat tire.
- You need invitations for a party.
- You spilled ink on your clothes.
- Your piano is out of tune.
- Your cat is up a tree and won't come down.
- There's a house on fire.

Make a telephone booth out of wood or a refrigerator cardboard box, or borrow a real one from the local telephone company. Install a toy telephone, a local directory, and a set of task cards using pictures and words to pose situations that need solving. A child chooses a card, decides whom to call, and looks up the number. Then he dials, reports his problem, and asks for assistance in solving it.

One child is chosen as a man-in-the-street interviewer. He plans a series of questions asking for opinions or facts on a topic of the day. The topic might be a current news item, school situation, or fantasy situation. Several other children assume an identity by dressing up in clothes from a dress-up box or corner, and are interviewed by the Man in the Street.

Ideas for Man-in-the-Street interviewers and Soapbox orators
- Should every child have his own room?
- Are parents really necessary?
- Should children have an allowance?
- Should the cafeteria have better food?
- Should children be allowed to play in the street?
- Should there be one president for children and another for adults in our country?
- Should children be able to put up signs that say "For Kids Only"?
- Should children be paid for working at school?
- Should parents leave children home alone?

Set up a Lost and Found box for things actually lost in the classroom or for things collected from children for this activity. A child takes an object from the box and gives clues about it or about its owner. Other children try to figure out to whom it belongs.

Prepare a wheel or chart of different types of parties, such as a tea party, a birthday party, a going-away party, and a New Year's party. One or two children plan for one of the parties and invite others to it. The children have the party, talking about where to sit, what they'd like to eat, and how they enjoyed it. Plans for the party can include making invitations, setting the table, preparing food or models of food, and making party favors.

List two or three currently popular films or TV programs on a chart or chalkboard. Have several children who have seen the same program get together to retell it, helping each other arrive at the correct sequence and details.

Children help fill shoe boxes or other containers with collections of objects based on a common situation or story. Individually or in small groups, children choose a collection and play act with the objects. Two or three boxes can be combined and used together. Vocabulary can be written on the box or lid as an aid to the children's imaginative play.

Set up a table, bookcase, or shelf as a museum with exhibits which will be changed every few days. One or two children set up a display and act as docents, giving information as other children tour the museum asking questions and making observations. Some display categories might be toy cars, shells, pencils and pens, balls, candy, or anything else the docents may choose.

Announcers

A child uses a top hat and a whistle as he pretends to be a circus ringmaster. He announces various acts that will be appearing in the circus. Picture cards or word cards provide ideas for the ringmaster to use in his announcements.

Make a set of rhyming word cards for children to use in making up cheerleader's yells and chants. Children use a megaphone to teach their chants to others in the class. They can also make up actions to go with their yells.

One child acts as an airport announcer, making up information about arrivals, departures, and delays by matching items from lists of cities, times, and flight numbers. He may tape his announcements for later replay, or other children could use toy or paper planes to "land" or "take off" as announcements are made.

The children and teacher make lists of names of sports teams, sports action words, and words that are synonyms for winning and losing. Children use the words to make up sports broadcasts which they announce over a microphone to an audience.

ANIMALS

Make a collection of animal pictures. One child chooses several pictures. He then acts out an animal parade by imitating the sounds each animal would make as it passed by. Another child names the animals in the order heard in the parade. Then he repeats the sounds in the same sequence the first child used.

Cut out or draw animals with one or more missing parts, such as a lion without a mane, a bird without wings and a beak, and a giraffe without a neck. A child chooses an animal and tells what is missing, using as many descriptive words for it as possible.

Collect several sound-makers such as a rattle, a jar filled with gravel, cellophane, and a paper bag with some walnuts inside. A child takes an object, discovers the noise it makes, and tells what kind of an animal might sound the same way. He then makes up a story to tell about the animal and its sounds.

Two children are chosen or volunteer to answer questions about animals. They decide which one of them will act as the "Lying Tamer," giving only fantasy or make-believe answers, and which will answer as the "Zoo Keeper," giving factual answers. Other children make up questions for the answer men, and, based on the answers given, try to guess who is the Lying Tamer and who is the Zoo Keeper.

Puppets

Collect junk items in multiples (10-20 screws, several pencils, bottle caps, etc.) and store in a bag, box, or any other convenient container. Using numbered hand puppets, children take turns reaching into the container and picking up the number of like objects corresponding to the number on their puppet.

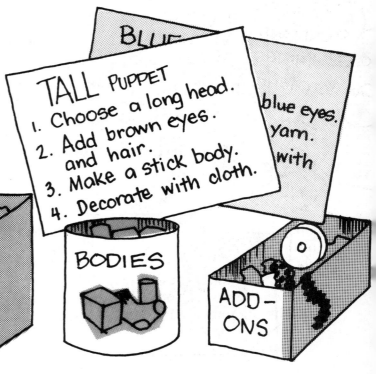

Set up parts boxes for children to use in making puppets. The HEADS box might contain light bulbs, gourds, balls, lids, and crackers. The BODIES box might have cartons, fabrics, socks, tubes. Accessories for decoration of the puppets can include buttons, beads, rick rack, etc. Children choose an idea card and follow directions to make that particular puppet (color puppet, number puppet, ethnic puppet, size puppet).

Design a set of task cards to use with puppets which give directions for movement using arrows, pictures, and words such as LEFT, RIGHT, UP, DOWN, THROUGH, BELOW, ABOVE. Children use the cards and invent dialogue for the puppets as they are moved in the manner described in the directions.

Make puppets for each basic shape: triangle, circle, square, rectangle. Involve children in collecting corresponding shape props to match each puppet. For example, the circle puppet's props might include a ball, ring, and assorted washers. Children use the puppet and props for play or develop skits and stories. Dialogue starter questions or picture cards may be developed.

Write name tags for pairs of opposite words. One child chooses a tag and hangs it around his puppet. A second child finds the opposite name tag for his puppet. They create dialogue to correspond to their name tags.

Make a chart showing pictures and words that suggest different ways of talking. Children roll dice, match the number to the chart, and use a puppet to do the talking in the style suggested.

Several different backdrop settings are painted or drawn by the teacher or children. Children choose a backdrop and puppets and create scenes and dialogue to match the setting.

Design programs for plays which give titles, scene descriptions, and a list of characters. Children choose a program and create scenery, puppets, and dialogue to go with the program.

5.
WRITING EXPERIENCES

writing (rīt'-ing) 1. *process of forming lines, symbols, letters or words*
2. *producing a communication*

Writing, as the term applies to this chapter, is any activity that helps to develop a child's motor and mental ability to express himself through written symbols. Learning how to write is as individualistic as a child's written product; therefore, the teacher should determine which writing activities best match the interests, needs, and developmental levels of the children.

Translating thoughts into symbols is one of the goals for using writing activities. A child is motivated to reach this goal when he has something to express. Real experiences stimulate the child to share or save what has happened to him by recording it in some type of written form which may show its beginnings in symbols and pictures. As the child writes or dictates, he gives meaning and understanding to the experience. He also sorts out the learnings and feelings he has from the experience. Writing is thus a means of helping the child communicate with both the inner and outer world in which he lives.

The teacher must make some important decisions regarding writing before she constructs and uses these writing activities. Her position in relationship to the following philosophical statements will ultimately determine the nature of the young child's experience with writing.

- Writing reinforces the learning of reading and speaking.
- Children should be taught the appropriateness of writing forms for varying situations.

- Expression in writing is more important than the mechanics of writing.
- The child's own need to communicate rather than a standardized or graded curriculum should dictate which skills will be taught.
- All writing activities do not need to be formally corrected.
- A child must have a purpose for what he has written in order to value his writing.

The writing activities shown in this chapter have been grouped into three types of learning centers: general materials center, general activity center, and centers organized around a theme.

General Materials Center for Writing

This type of center is an area in the room containing a variety of paper, writing tools, and supplies. Children use this area when a need for writing occurs. The type of written communication or the skill a child is working on will determine the materials a child will select. The replacement of expendable items and the care of all materials should be assigned to the class so that the center is constantly ready for use.

Word Lists For Children to Use as References	**Book Titles**
• Color Words	• Yummy Book
• Number Words	• Yechhhh!
• Days/Months /Holidays of the Year	• Wheels
• Size Words	• WOW!
• Family Words	• Help!
• Play Words	• Money
• Animal Words	• Sobs and Tears
• Food Words	• I Could Scream
• Sound Words	• I Dig Music
• Helping Words	• Store
• Words Used a Lot	• P.S.: Wish We Were Here
	• It's Brand New

General Activity Center for Writing

An assortment of activities aimed at helping children develop and practice writing skills is located in this center. These activities are generally based on motivational gimmicks to encourage writing practice. They also provide those children who do not have topics for writing with ideas. In addition to the activities the center also houses a supply of materials for writing.

Scribe's Corner

Children use carbon paper to make copies as they write stories or practice letter formation. Copies can be added to a class file or book of stories, taken home for sharing with families, or given to another child to edit or illustrate.

Older children or the teacher carve pictograph sentences or stories on plaster of Paris or clay tablets. Other children translate the sentences or stories into words.

Many kinds of wrapping paper are collected by the teacher and children. The collection can include birthday, Christmas, shower, baby, and wedding papers, brown bags, and bags from various stores. Children choose a piece of the paper and write a story on it, using the designs and illustrations on the paper as clues and ideas for writing. Vocabulary for stories can be made available to children by wrapping a box in a piece of paper and writing appropriate words on it.

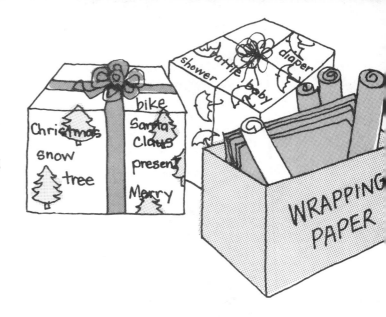

Children write a story in a box lid, which has been cut at each corner so it will lay flat. Then they frame their story by drawing around the edges of the box lid illustrations for all or parts of it. The framed stories can be hung in a classroom story gallery.

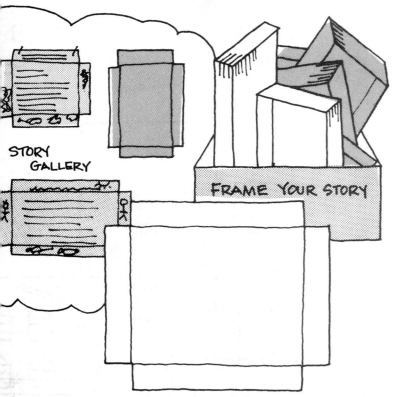

Children practice letter formation by tracing over words on boxes and labels from cans.

Children play the role of a secretary by transcribing a teacher-made tape of simple sentences. Props such as glasses, a stenographer's pad, and several kinds of pencils add interest to this activity.

Collect many different objects which can be used with paint or ink for writing. Children practice writing letters with different objects and compare the results. They can also choose an object and write a story about it. Some objects to include are a feather, leaf, bone, straw, pastry wheel, cake cutter, comb, screw, and nail.

With the children, make a chart categorizing the letters of the alphabet according to shapes or strokes. The letters m, n, and h might be "humps," and the letters z, l, t, w, and x, "stripes." Make animal worksheets to correspond to letter families the group has chosen. Children practice writing letters by filling in the worksheets with the matching letters.

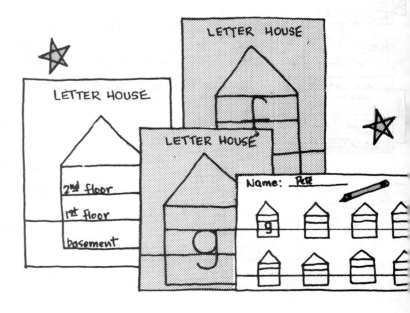

The teacher prepares a set of cards with one letter in each house. Children choose a card, study the letter's placement on the lines, and practice writing the letter on a worksheet.

ICE CREAM CENTER

. . . an example of related activities organized into a learning center

Using a chart of real and make-believe names of ice cream flavors as a reference, children find the word that fits the configuration pattern illustrated on the ice cream cone. Ice cream cones showing various configuration patterns are run off on dittoed worksheets.

A number of incomplete pictures of ice cream cones are dittoed for children to use. Children trace the partially drawn cones and complete them.

Words that describe ice cream are written on cards. Children use three words to write an advertisement for selling ice cream.

Ice Cream Center

Make two sets of cards, one showing numerals, the other showing titles for ice cream stories. Children draw one from each set and paste them onto an ice cream ditto or cutout. Then they compose and write or dictate a sentence or story to go with the title containing the corresponding number of words.

Make a chart using paper circles or plates for the ice cream and real cones. Write directions on the chart. Children use a worksheet that has cones drawn on it and fill in the sheet according to the directions on the chart.

Using the worksheet, children rewrite the words in all capital or all lowercase letters.

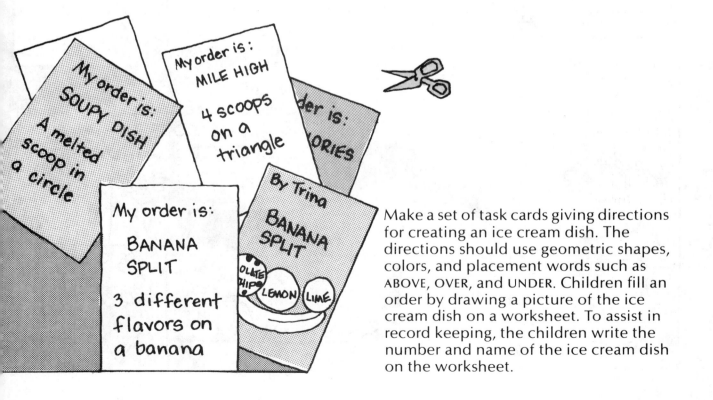

Make a set of task cards giving directions for creating an ice cream dish. The directions should use geometric shapes, colors, and placement words such as ABOVE, OVER, and UNDER. Children fill an order by drawing a picture of the ice cream dish on a worksheet. To assist in record keeping, the children write the number and name of the ice cream dish on the worksheet.

MONSTERS

To set up monster activities as a learning center, section off an area of the room to display the activities. Some suggestions for displaying the activities as a center are:

- Build a monster cave out of cardboard and locate the activities inside it.
- Make a wire frame or papier-mâché monster and attach the activities to it.
- Cut out a large mouth of a monster and place the activities inside.
- Paint a monstrous backdrop to pin the activities on.

Collect as references and resources for the center:

- Plastic and paper toy models of monsters
- Advertisements for monster movies and television programs
- Monster masks
- Makeup and wigs

Who
bites
necks?

Dracula
bites
necks.

The two-headed monster holds questions in one head and answers in the other. Children find a matching question and answer and copy them on the corresponding side of a ditto, using the correct punctuation. Children can help write or dictate questions and answers for the monsters.

I have
4 legs,
3 eyes,
and 2 tails.
I eat trees.

by Cindy

The Who Am I? box contains large footprints cut out in various shapes. Clues are written on each footprint. Children choose a footprint, draw an imaginary monster according to the clues, and label the parts of the monster.

I have
legs toes

WHO AM I?

Monsters

The teacher prepares papers with two or three letters printed on them. Children trace over the letters several times and then make them into a monster picture.

by Pedro

The teacher prepares patterns of the heads of animals and the bodies of people. Children choose one head and one body, trace around them, cut them out, and paste them together to make a monster. They name the monster and write its name on a name tag which has a large box drawn on it as a reminder to capitalize the first letter of the name.

Porcina

Children learn to make charts by applying simple guidelines as they design and construct monster charts. Make a "How To" chart and a list of possible titles for children to work from.

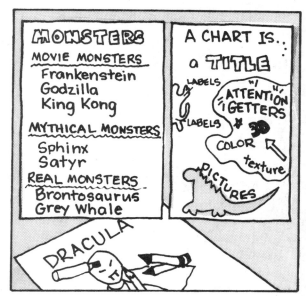

MONSTERS
MOVIE MONSTERS
Frankenstein
Godzilla
King Kong
MYTHICAL MONSTERS
Sphinx
Satyr
REAL MONSTERS
Brontosaurus
Grey Whale

A CHART IS...
a TITLE
LABELS
LABELS
ATTENTION GETTERS
COLOR
texture
PICTURES

DRACULA

Start and add to a Monstrous Words chart. Use names of monsters, long words, and monstrous-meaning words. Children copy words on large or long pieces of paper and try to use words in dictation, sharing, stories, and drawings.

CHORES
sweep
mow the lawn
vacuum   mop
dust   weed
□lish   wash

MONSTERS

One large monster with super-sharp... to mow the law...

MONSTROUS
WORDS
snarling   huge

SUPERCALIFRAGILISTICEXP

BRONT...

Gigantor
Gigantor

Make a chart of tasks and everyday chores and a collection of monster cutouts and pictures. Children match a chore with a monster which could do it well and draw or write about it. They could also design want ads for the jobs.

Children make up monster menus. They may include food names that: (1) begin with the same letter as the monster name, (2) have the same number of syllables, (3) are actually associated with the monster, (4) go with the monster in some imaginative way. Menus could be used for monster parties.

KING KONG KNISH

GRIFFIN GOULASH

MONSTER MUSH

SEA SERPENT SUSHI

GODZILLA GARBANZOS

TYRANNOSAURUS TAMALES

DRACULA DRUMSTICKS

BLOB BAGELS

HOLIDAYS

To set up as a center:
- Designate a permanent area in the room for the center.
- Select from the collection of activities those that are most appropriate for the month. Add activities to the center for the holidays of each succeeding month.

Pads of paper are stapled to a pocket chart along the pocket strip. Holiday sentences are made of individual word cards, and each sentence is placed in a separate packet. Capital letters are omitted. The child selects a packet and arranges the words in the pocket chart to form a sentence. He places each word next to one of the pads of paper. He then writes the capitals that are needed on the pads. The child can copy the sentence for practice in handwriting or for assessment and record-keeping purposes.

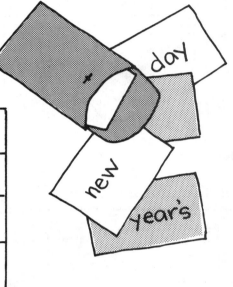

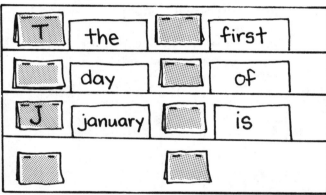

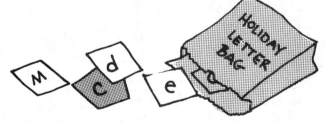

A collection of holiday decals or seals is placed in a paper bag. Letters are made on cards and placed in another bag. From the bags children randomly select a holiday seal and five letters. They glue the seal at the top of a paper and write the letters down the side of the paper. Then they find or think of words beginning with these letters to describe or go with the seal.

Holidays

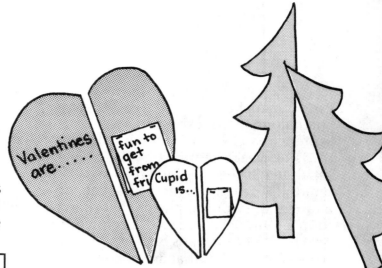

Prepare a ditto for the month. Children fill in the calendar according to the clues presented on a task card. Each task card should name the holiday and give ample clues for completing the calendar.

More Ideas for Holiday Task Cards
- Computation: adding, subtracting, multiplying, dividing
- Locating points on a grid: three columns across, four rows down
- Counting by any multiple of numbers
- Tell date and give clues for the holiday: on the 25th a jolly man arrives
- Ordinal number clues: third Thursday in the month
- Roman numerals: Valentine's Day is on XIV

Objects that characterize holidays are made in a variety of sizes and cut in half. An incomplete sentence, paragraph, or story is written by the teacher on one half of the object. Paper is attached to the other half. A student finds two matching halves and completes the sentence, paragraph, or story.

Mount several headlines on a bulletin board or chart. Under each headline attach a pad of paper. Put holiday objects in a container labeled "News Room." Children choose an object from the News Room and write a news story about it under a headline. The story will contain ideas about both the headline and the object.

HOLIDAY : Christmas	
FACT	**FICTION**
Christmas is always on December 25ᵗʰ.	Santa Claus got stuck in the chimney.

Make holiday dittos or large charts. Children choose one and write, draw, or dictate and recopy fact and fantasy events for the holiday.

Draw or paste a picture of a holiday symbol in one of the squares of 2-inch square graph paper. Children write a sentence using the name of the holiday symbol in it. The sentence must be planned so that the picture is in place as a substitute for the word. Changing the placement of the picture on the paper will cause children to change the sentence structure.

My	basket	was	filled
on	Easter	by	🐰
He	gave	me	lots
of	candy.		By Genes.

Columbus went to sea and discovered America.

by Gail

Make decks of cards with names of famous holiday celebrities, their accomplishments, and the settings of their accomplishments. Children find the cards that match from each of the three decks. After completing the match, the student writes a sentence about the holiday using all three elements.

6.
EXPERIENCES IN THE ARTS

Developing a child's awareness and appreciation of the arts should be as integral a part of the curriculum as is developing fundamental skills. While art experiences expose children to aesthetics, they also provide opportunities for participation in a variety of expressive forms. The total involvement offered by an art experience encourages the use of sensory, intrapersonal, and physical aspects of the child's being. The child's verbal and physical interpretations of an art experience reinforce his affective growth and help him relate the understandings gained to other people and the world around him.

In using the art activities in this chapter, the teacher may wish to plan an initial or introductory experience to motivate and prepare children to self-select from the array of activities placed within the classroom environment. Field trips, audiovisual aids, and resource people can be used with the total class in an introductory art experience. Other staff members, community and parent experts, and talented students from the school can often provide experiences the teacher may be hesitant or unable to provide herself.

The following activities are options for children to choose from as a result of an interest that emerges from an initial large group art experience. These activities might be placed collectively in the room as a learning center. When used in this manner, the teacher must provide the explanations necessary to enable children to perform the tasks independently. Another approach to using these activities is to consider them as individual, unrelated experiences or as single follow-up activities to be used by the teacher or to be chosen by students.

The home-school relationship is strengthened when family participation is seen as a necessary link in the learning experience. The family can continue and expand an experience for a child by doing such things as attending concerts, visiting museums, and talking to local artists and craftsmen. Lists sent home to announce the ways parents can assist in the learning process should include the following:

- Visiting local art galleries and museums
- Reading the cultural and local events section of the newspaper
- Visiting a variety of theaters
- Browsing through books in libraries and book stores which contain information about the arts
- Going to stores which specialize in art supplies, musical instruments, and dance attire
- Visiting local private schools which specialize in art lessons
- Speaking with artists and craftsmen at open-air galleries and book faires
- Becoming familiar with stories of artists' lives
- Touring art studios, shops, and factories
- Surveying the yellow pages of the telephone book for art stores, art dealers, and drama or music teachers
- Finding out about the type of activities offered by recreation departments and at universities and playgrounds
- Attending rehearsals of the symphony and other musical groups, dance ensembles, and dramatic performances

Painting and Sculpture

Children make a Mondrian-style picture by creating an arrangement of paper rectangles and squares of different sizes and colors.

Children look for the common subject of many different works of art. Then they categorize the works according to certain qualities of the subject. For example, many different suns can be found in art which could be categorized according to cool, warm, tropical, etc. Many animals can be found which might then be categorized as cartoon-like, realistic, geometric, etc.

Children choose objects, such as toys, blocks, and fabric swatches, from a collection provided at the center. They use the objects to translate a two-dimensional painting into a three-dimensional model.

Prepare several placemats with regular and irregular colored shapes. Provide varying lengths and colors of string for children to weave among the shapes in a Miro style.

Make a set of cards of words that could describe a body such as thin, heavy, portly, and angular. Children match the cards to people portrayed by artists such as Rubens, Giacometti, Modigliani, Picasso, and primitive artists.

Children choose a famous work of art and reproduce it in some way. They may change one characteristic of the work and try to leave the others the same, or they may try to copy it exactly.

by David

Painting and Sculpture

Children make cardboard box buildings and design and paint murals on them. Diego Rivera, local muralists, and others are used as examples. Other children may discuss the message or intent of the mural.

Using many kinds of junk, such as springs, gears, string, straws, old appliance and machine parts, and motors and batteries, children create their own kinetic art piece.

Set up a display of models or pictures of famous sculptures. Children choose a sculpture and put themselves into the same body shape.

Set up a display of prints of still lifes, landscapes, and abstract paintings. Children use toys, junk, and objects from nature to match to appropriate prints. They can then share their reasoning with others.

Children choose a famous work and use it as the basis for an advertisement. For example, they might choose a photo of a Calder mobile and use it to design an advertisement for weathervanes.

Children choose a picture and then dress a doll to go with the picture. If people are shown, children might try to duplicate the costume.

Children use the idea of Picasso's Blue Period as a starting point for creating their own series of pictures based on a color.

Children choose a famous picture or sculpture of people. They try to recreate the scene by making costumes, props, using makeup, and arranging themselves like the subjects of the art piece.

After looking at numerous films, photos, and books of other countries, children create a World Fair. Each child or group designs and builds a pavilion in the architectural style of the country they choose.

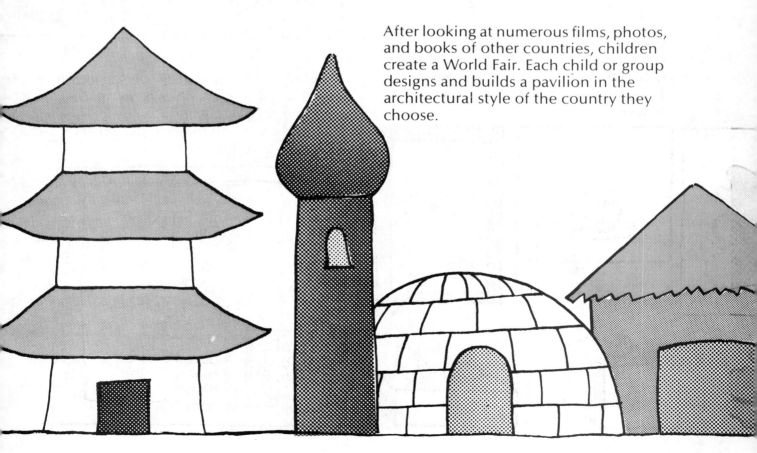

Body Movement

Some of these activities can be varied by musical accompaniment and by the use of such things as blindfolds, scarves, flags, streamers, sticks, balls, and other props.

Children space themselves around an area either singly or in pairs. As the teacher calls out a word or shows a picture card, children put their bodies in a matching shape or position. As another word is indicated, the children move into a new shape. Pairs of words, or several words in a series may be used. Some words to start with:

pretzel—spaghetti
crisp—soggy
angry—calm

Draw mazes on oilcloth, butcher paper, or with chalk on the floor. Children choose or can be told an emotion word such as anger, fear, happiness, or sadness. They move through the mazes as they try to portray the emotion.

Cut out a large number of foot patterns. The footprints are arranged in patterns for children to follow. Variations for the course can include sideways and backwards steps; steps over low chairs, boxes, and other obstacles; and steps close and far apart. Music and clapped rhythm patterns can accompany the children's movements.

Cut various sizes and shapes of large paper. Each child chooses a paper and, as the teacher or another child calls out the name of an object, tries to completely fill the paper with his body in the shape of the object. Children can exchange papers before each new object is called.

Arrange many children in a seating arrangement simulating an orchestra. Sections are named for body parts. One child "conducts" the orchestra as a musical selection is played. Orchestra members move the designated body part to the music as cued by the conductor.

Children move between two or more points marked on the floor, imitating the movements of such things as a tree, airplane, bouncing ball, kite, triangle, and swing.

Assemble a set of picture or word cards of objects such as paper, tree, puddle, ice cream. Make a spinner showing weather words. Children choose an object card, spin the spinner, and use their bodies to portray the object as it might appear in the weather shown on the spinner.

One child assumes a pose. A second child faces him and mirrors the pose. Variations might include copying the pose from different angles (side, back to back) and mirroring poses of figures drawn on giant sized cards.

MUSIC

Children listen to many selections of music and choose one to go with a favorite story, rhyme, or poem. They may play the music while they read the selection, or they may tape the two for others to hear.

Children use time groups such as long ago, today, and in the future, and early morning, afternoon, and late at night to categorize music selections. One extension of this activity would be to have children make up their own music to fit into the different categories.

Children make a favorite fairy tale, poem, or child-authored story into a musical play.

Children create travel posters of a location suggested by a musical selection's mood, composer, or style.

Write simple directions of steps on cards. Children choose a card and do the steps in a repeated pattern to the march music of Sousa or others.

| 5 steps forward |
| 3 in place |

| 3 steps right |
| ½ turn |
| 3 steps left |

Individually or in small groups children make up questions to ask others after listening to a piece of music.

Set up a private corner of the room or construct a listening booth from a refrigerator carton, wood, or cardboard pieces, which is large enough to accommodate one child and his actions. Place inside a collection of things such as pinwheels, crepe paper streamers, scarves, flashlights, and toys with moving parts, which a child may use to accompany a musical selection he chooses to listen to.

With children's help make up a set of large cards showing various lines or symbols that can represent tempos, rhythms, pitch, and dynamics (loudness or softness). Children may use them while listening to a piece of music or may try to reconstruct the progress of the music after a listening experience.

7.
ENVIRONMENTAL EXPERIENCES

The whole world is a classroom. Everything in the world is a resource for learning. Every environmental experience provides a curriculum.

The concept that the structure of a classroom is the center of learning is as outdated as the concept that the teacher is the sole transmitter of knowledge. The boundaries between the school and the outside world must be eradicated in order to expand the opportunities for learning about the world by learning in the world. In achieving this end, the learning environment is perceived as the total community, and the school is considered to be one part of this community.

Adopting an environmental program necessitates changes in the use of the classroom. In environmental studies the classroom becomes the place where interest is sparked, need is expressed, resource possibilities are outlined, plans are made, and follow-up study and experiments are done. The environment becomes the information-gathering source. It is through the students' interaction with an observation of the environment that data are collected, firsthand learnings are obtained, ideas for classroom activities are generated, and motivation and interest in learning are stimulated. Combining classroom and environmental learning activities enables students to integrate subject matter content with real experiences.

There is no set pattern for utilizing the environment as a learning tool. Exploration and use of the environment can stem from a classroom activity, an exploratory trip to a locale, or from children's experiences in their environment (outside school time). Also, it is not necessary for all students to visit the same environmental site at the same time. Flexibility in scheduling visits for individuals or small groups of students can be achieved by using parents, instructional aides, or secondary students as environmental "teachers." The classroom teacher should plan for the possibility of more than one visit to an environmental site in order to encourage the continuity of the learning process.

The methods employed by the teacher to prepare students for experiences in the environment will depend on the goals she sets for the activity.

Goal	Preparation
Exploration: Experiences to stimulate the children's awareness and initiate possibilities for self-selected learning activities.	• Discussing and practicing observational techniques. • Teaching and reviewing sensory awareness skills. • Providing for simple record keeping by means of photographs, drawings, graphs, notes.
Data Gathering: Opportunities to use the environment as an information source.	• Learning interviewing techniques. • Introducing and practicing recording skills, such as note-taking, collecting, illustrating. • Preparing materials needed, such as questions, graphs, notebooks, measuring equipment.
Skill Development: Activities that use the environment for teaching, practicing, and extending basic skills.	• Introducing skills to be used. • Collecting necessary materials.

Before taking students to environmental locations, the teacher should do some preliminary planning. Any or all of these steps might be done with the help of children, parents, or aides:

Visiting the site or telephoning to check these items:

- safety features
- route to and from site
- individuals most receptive to children and most knowledgeable in the subject

Accumulating necessary materials:

- paper, graphs, pencils, felt pens, cameras, film, tape recorders for record keeping
- bags, boxes, or jars for collecting objects at the site
- bike bags, plastic buckets, wash bins, wire racks, plastic or paper shopping bags for carrying
- safety pins, band-aids, extra money, telephone numbers in case of emergencies

Contacting parents to inform them of

- purpose of the experience
- needs parents can fill
- possible places parents can take children to augment the experience

The follow-up activities that take place in the classroom after the environmental experience may need more structuring. Materials and space to work on projects or activities must be designated. Because, ideally, environmental experiences become the basis of the child's curriculum, the teacher must plan ways to design the total classroom program around them or, at least, to be sure adequate time, space, and materials are allowed for environmental and follow-up activities. In this way environmental studies will be relevant and meaningful for students.

Hamburger Stand

Design a new logo.

Hot Dog · · · 35¢
Chili Dog · · 50¢
Plain Burger 50¢
Super Burger 85¢

Find out the time needed to prepare different hamburgers and other food.

List machines from your kitchen that correspond to those found at the stand.

Design new uniforms for employees.

Use discarded containers to build a model of a food stand.

Research the weight of meat in different kinds of hamburgers.

Take photographs of people eating or waiting in line at the stand. Categorize them according to facial expression, body position, manner of eating, etc.

Make cartoons of hamburgers and hot dogs. Give them personalities.

Make a collection of hamburger recipes.

Write the corporation for information about franchise regulations, prices, etc.

Make a rating scale to survey people's reactions to taste, price, size, etc. of foods sold at the stand.

Make ketchup in the classroom using the label on the bottle as a source of ingredients.

Be an efficiency expert. Find a way to cut the number of employees, the time for service, the cost of food.

Find out about clean-up procedures.

Have a blindfolded child smell foods and guess what they are.

Write descriptions of various foods from their smells.

Make a collage showing the source of each part of a hamburger.

Design a favorite food stand.

Survey to find the number of bites needed to eat the different kinds of hamburgers.

Write food orders for classmates on real or student-created order forms.

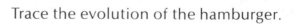

Trace the evolution of the hamburger.

Make up a new relish in the classroom.

Count how many french fries are in bags of various sizes.

Cut a potato to find out how many french fries can be made.

Count the number of sesame seeds on a bun. Place seeds or other objects on a paper outline of the bun to show the number counted.

THE NURSERY

Independent study

- Write to seed and other companies advertising in magazines and newspapers for information about plants.
- Learn when different flowers bloom. Make a time strip showing the months of the year and the flowers that bloom during each month.
- Make a nursery of unusual plants such as the Venus fly trap and the artillery plant.
- Examine insects and other garden pests with a magnifying glass and microscope. Find out how these affect plants and what will eliminate them.

Interview nursery employees

- to find out the schedules for plant care. Make one for the classroom plant shop.
- to get information for writing a *Farmer's Almanac*.
- to find out how to compare the anatomy or "birth" of a plant to that of a human being.

Collect

- samples of plants from children's homes and take them to the nursery to be identified. Make a book of *My Plants at Home*.
- plant parts and categorize according to leaf shape, color, vein pattern, flowers, etc.
- plastic tag markers from the nursery to use for vocabulary building, sorting, syllabication, and word derivation study.

Create

- a replica of a plant for the classroom plant shop
- a garden or area of a garden and compute the cost of all the materials
- pictures of clichés using plant words such as green thumb, growing like a weed, and a rolling stone gathers no moss
- cartoons showing conversation between plants
- plant or flower arrangements by cutting out and pasting pictures from garden magazines such as *Sunset*
- a map of a nursery
- pictures of plants to resemble their names such as "string of pearls," "baby tears," and "weeping willow"
- new names for plants based on appearance such as calling a fuchsia a ballerina

Recycle junk to make

- gardening tools
- a dish garden
- a trellis
- a plant container

Experiment with

- organic gardening. Try various techniques in the classroom or at home.
- pesticides and plant foods. Study the effects of different ones on plants.
- turning various plants away from the sun to see how long the leaves take to turn toward it again.

SHOPPING CENTER

Design and create
- a new shopping cart
- a new bag for a store
- a new sign
- other layouts for a shopping center
- a new shopping center
- a new product for a store
- additions to make the shopping center more enjoyable (i.e., kiddie playground)
- a project to enhance the center such as planting an area, painting trash cans, cleaning up, sidewalk murals—then really do it!

Independent study
- compare two shopping centers
- study the process of producing a product
- learn about workers' pay, training, jobs

Collect menus, sale sheets, advertisements. Use for vocabulary building.

Money
- compare prices in different stores for the same object
- find items that match the prices on the sales slips
- count out the money shown on a sales slip
- find items in ads which could be bought with given amounts of play or real money in change purses or envelopes

Collect bags from various stores. Use as containers to classify words, objects, sales slips, etc. pertaining to each store.

Interview merchants
- to get answers for questions
- to get samples of materials
- to find out which ones will visit school as resource people

Tape
- sounds
- dialogue between customers and sales clerks

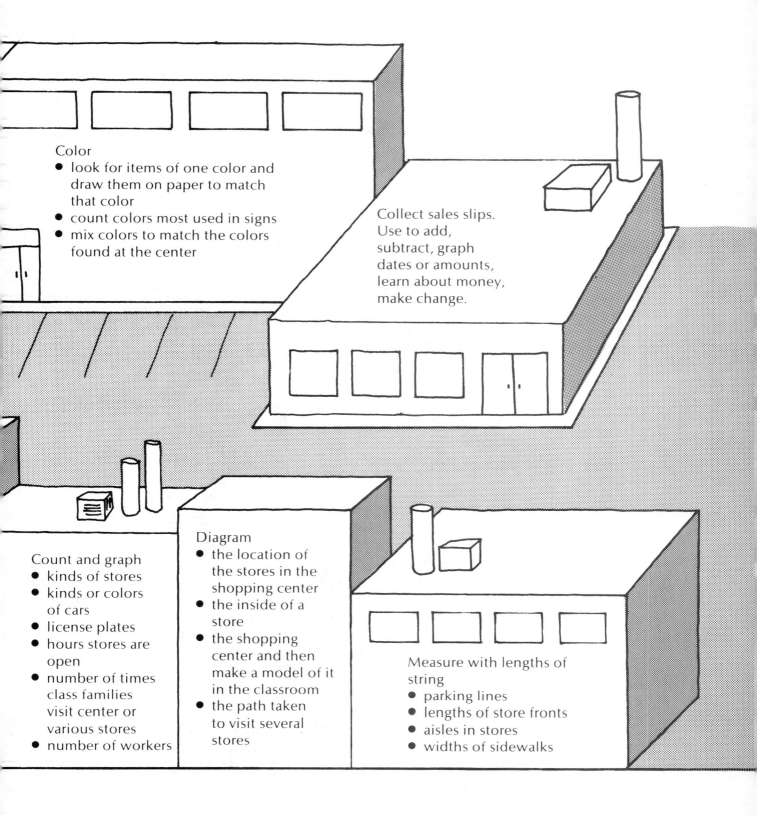

Color
- look for items of one color and draw them on paper to match that color
- count colors most used in signs
- mix colors to match the colors found at the center

Collect sales slips. Use to add, subtract, graph dates or amounts, learn about money, make change.

Count and graph
- kinds of stores
- kinds or colors of cars
- license plates
- hours stores are open
- number of times class families visit center or various stores
- number of workers

Diagram
- the location of the stores in the shopping center
- the inside of a store
- the shopping center and then make a model of it in the classroom
- the path taken to visit several stores

Measure with lengths of string
- parking lines
- lengths of store fronts
- aisles in stores
- widths of sidewalks

The World Around Me

SIT IN THE MIDDLE OF ANY PLACE

Make your world larger or smaller with art media.

Categorize things in groups by size, origin, shape, mobility, natural versus man-made.

Repeat a pattern seen in your world.

Collect several objects. Drop them from a standing position to find out which hits the ground the fastest, slowest, loudest, etc.

Lay out a string grid over one or two feet of your world. Reproduce this area on graph paper, drawing in objects as they appear in the string grid.

Finish a sign that reads, "This Land Is Good for _____."

Bring along a bag of words. Find things in your world that would go with one or more of the words.

Gather 5 objects. Glue them together to make something that shows where your world is located.

Write or tape stories entitled "How I Got Here," "All Around Me," "A Hundred Things," etc.

Pick out the closest and farthest points you can see, and show all the things you see in between.

Mark a point on the ground. Circle to the right or left and draw or tell all the things you have seen.

Write directions for how to find the site.

Choose any object. Count all the things you find that are the same as the first.

Design a landmark for your world.

Make up and fill out a squatter's rights form for your piece of the world.

Make a model of a building or house to cover an area of your world using materials found in that environment.

Take something, being careful not to hurt a living thing, from the outside environment and try growing it indoors.

Measure the area with parts of your body: hands, feet, thumbs, little finger. Record your findings.

Sift the area with different sizes of screens. Make a collection of objects found in each screen.

Use found items to create an instrument. Make up a song to sing about the area, or play one on your instrument.

Make up and do math problems using objects you find around you.

Mark a trail for someone else to follow into your world. Be careful not to damage the environment as you mark your path.

FACTORY

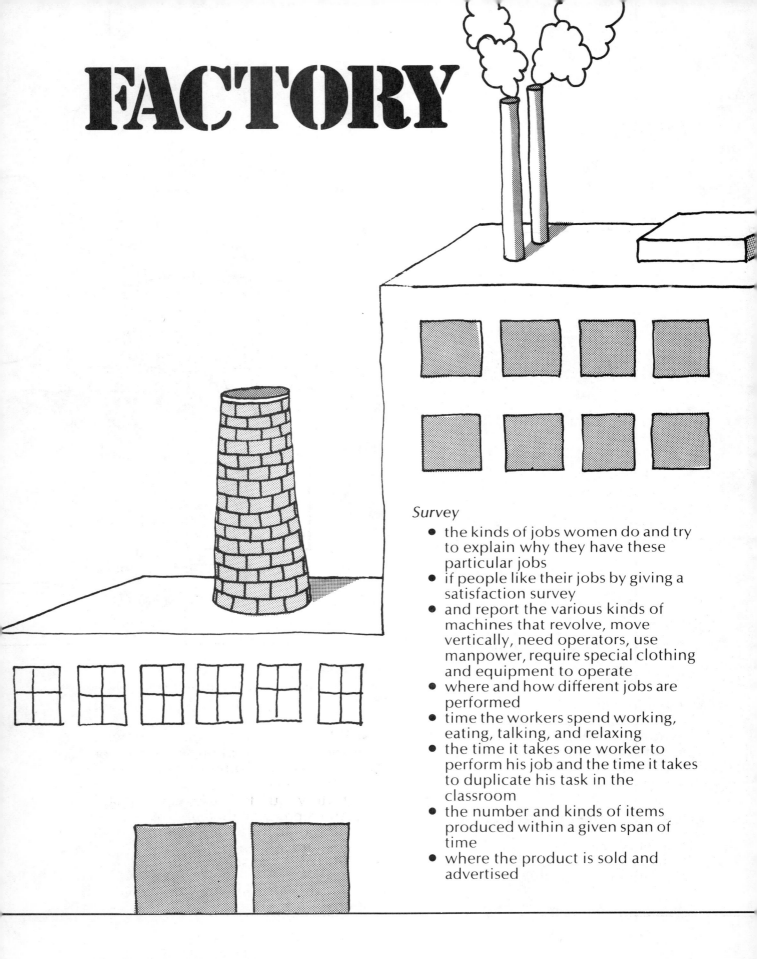

Survey

- the kinds of jobs women do and try to explain why they have these particular jobs
- if people like their jobs by giving a satisfaction survey
- and report the various kinds of machines that revolve, move vertically, need operators, use manpower, require special clothing and equipment to operate
- where and how different jobs are performed
- time the workers spend working, eating, talking, and relaxing
- the time it takes one worker to perform his job and the time it takes to duplicate his task in the classroom
- the number and kinds of items produced within a given span of time
- where the product is sold and advertised

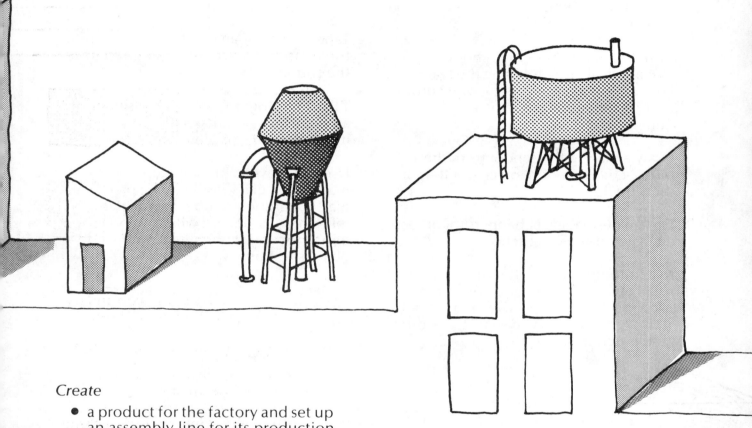

Create

- a product for the factory and set up an assembly line for its production
- reproductions of signs that workers need to read
- a color picture of the factory by using marking pens on a black and white photo taken at the site
- a model showing improvements for the factory
- new facilities and machines for the factory
- a comparison of facilities for workers in different factories
- a set of safety rules for the factory
- an incentive plan for increasing salaries or production

Collect

- forms, samples of products and materials, and other objects and set up a display
- factory sounds on a tape recorder and reproduce them in the classroom using various objects and instruments
- numbers you see posted in the factory

Outside the Door
Inside the Fence

Select and beautify an area with real or child-made objects.

Keep an animal or plant alive inside the room using things collected from outside.

Collect something that begins with each letter of the alphabet.

Visit all the rooms in the school in alphabetical order by using the teachers' last names; or order your visits according to the room numbers in reverse numerical order.

Draw a plan of the school from the perspective of a bird, piece of litter, or sack lunch.

Design new labels or banners for objects and sites around the school.

Match things outside the room to swatches of material or color cards.

Sit in a given area and describe it to other children in the area.

Experiment with puddles to determine the length of time they take to evaporate, and to find differences between those found on cement, grass, sand, and dirt.

Use precut lengths of string to estimate which outside objects would be the same lengths, and then prove the estimates by matching the strings to the objects.

Tape sounds of an outside area and play them inside for others to guess where the sounds were recorded.

Take a photograph showing just part of an object found outside the room. Give it to others to complete.

Use a Surveyor's Kit made up of a magnifying glass, cellophane, pieces of plastic, cardboard tubes, binoculars, telescope, cardboard with a pinhole, and mirror to look at and illustrate outside objects in a new way.

Collect and classify objects according to whether they were found in odd or even numbers at a given site.

Use outdoor equipment and objects to create simple machines such as levers, pulleys, and inclined planes.

With written or oral instructions direct children to where their names have been written outside the room.

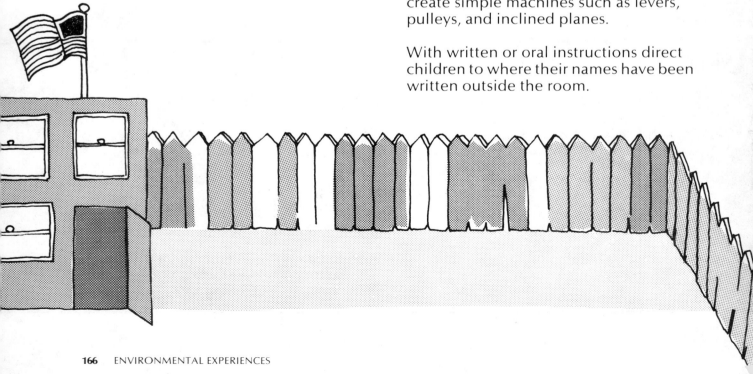

Add To, Improve, Change Your Environment

- In discussing and adding to these possibilities with children, help them understand the need for permission and adult assistance where appropriate.

Find places to plant to improve appearance, or to create a shade area or animal shelter.

Paint murals on unsightly fences, walls, or posts.

Design and make posters and ads for store windows.

Paint foot-shaped direction indicators on walks in front of stores, food stands, or gates to help solve pedestrian congestion.

Decorate garbage pails and trash containers around the neighborhood.

Ask a carpet store for remnants or old samples and piece them together to cover a section of the patio, driveway, or porch.

Create wood, metal, clay, or styrofoam house numbers or plaques to give to family members and neighbors.

Design, decorate, and distribute bottle, aluminum can, and newspaper collecting containers for neighbors to use for storing recyclable junk.

Make colorful bands of paper or fabric and attach them to telephone poles.

Draw a sidewalk hopscotch, marble, or 4-square design in colored, rather than white, chalk.

Ask a friend to help remove dead leaves or weeds from a lawn or planter. Plan a surprise for the person who helps with the job.

Paint designs on smooth rocks for a garden that needs cheering up.

Make a survey of things neighbors would like to see changed in the area. Find a way to make some of the changes.

Make a list of nuisances and safety hazards such as broken curbs and sidewalks, blind corners, and frayed wires and notify the proper state, city, or county agency.

Improve a room in the house with a new plant, rock garden, wall hanging, or other decoration.

Organize a neighborhood social event, such as a Saturday bike ride to a local park, a backyard picnic or barbecue, or a pet show.

Ask neighbors' permission to use number stencils and glow paint to revitalize their address numbers on the curb.

Weave a colorful God's eye, circle, or other design in a section of unsightly chain link fence.

TASK CARDS AND WORKSHEETS

*This worksheet is intended for teacher use. Teachers may run off one copy for each letter to be learned and then display the sheet with the appropriate letter on a bulletin board or elsewhere in the classroom. The corresponding student worksheet appears on page 225.

Find these crackers

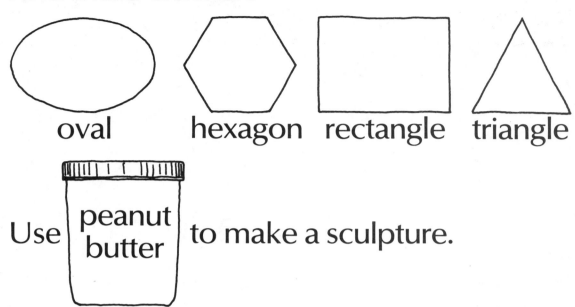

oval   hexagon   rectangle   triangle

Use **peanut butter** to make a sculpture.

Have some friends make one like yours and have a party.

- Find   6 circle crackers

           3 triangle crackers

           2 oval crackers

           2 hexagon crackers

- Stick them on a paper plate with peanut butter.

- Serve it to a friend.

•Find

3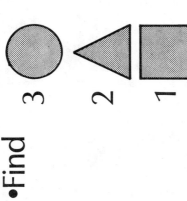

2

1

•Put them together to make
something that moves.

•Take a
picture of it.

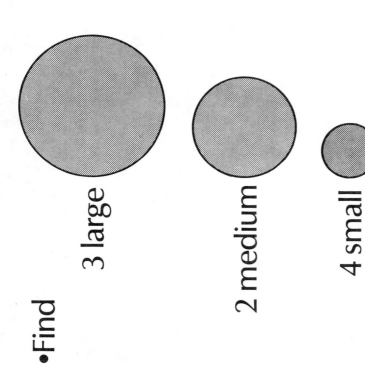

•Find

3 large

2 medium

4 small

•Put them together to make
something that moves in circles.

•Show it to a circle of friends.

Count out 10 pieces of junk.

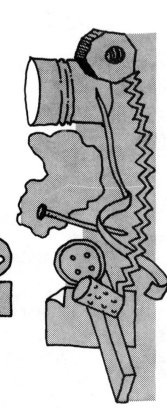

Put them in groups of 5 .

Build something different with each group.

Share it with the class in 10 minutes.

Pick up a handful of junk in your right hand.

Pick up a handful of junk in your left hand.

- Guess which hand has more.
- Count to prove your answer.
  - Tell a friend.

Count out this many

pieces of junk.

Have a friend
get an equal number.

Put your junk together
and make something.

Take it to another classroom.

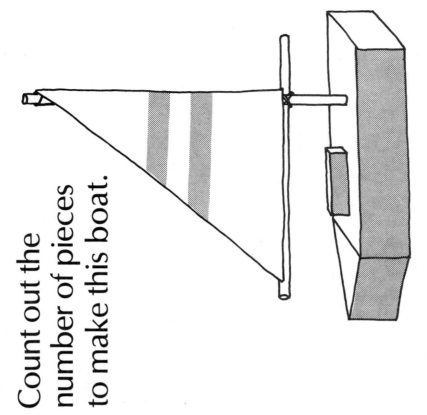

Count out the
number of pieces
to make this boat.

Find 4 more pieces of junk.

Put all the pieces together
to make a new kind of boat.

FIND AND FINISH

Find these.

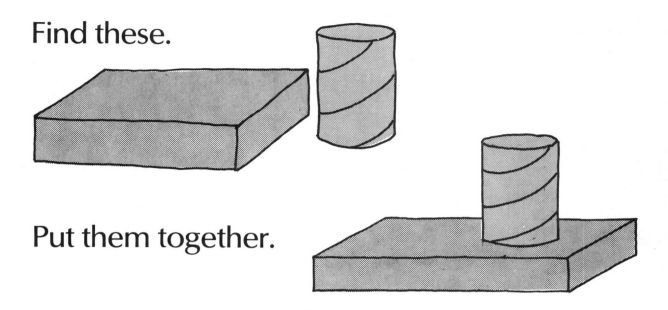

Put them together.

Finish it to make something to live in.

FIND AND FINISH

Find these.

Put them together.

Finish it to make something that moves.

COPY AND FINISH

Copy this.

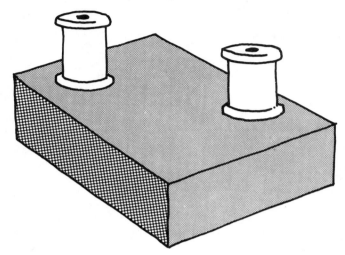

Finish it to make something for an astronaut.

COPY AND FINISH

Copy this.

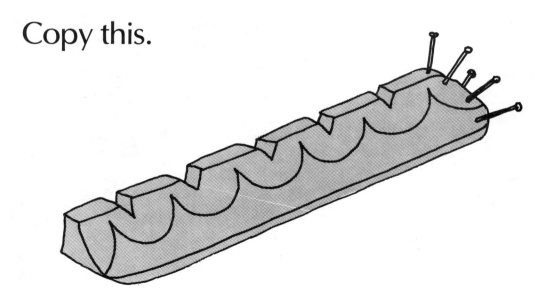

Finish it to make a crazy animal.

COPY AND FINISH

Copy this.

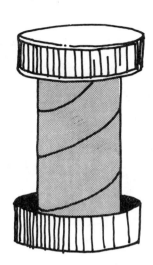

Finish it. What will you make?

Choose 4 things you can eat.

Choose 3 containers
that once held food.

Build a food store.

Use it to play store.

Choose 6 paper things.

Choose 5 metal things.

Choose 1 plastic thing.

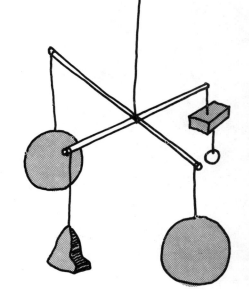

Build something that hangs.

Hang it in the room.

Choose 2 objects from nature.

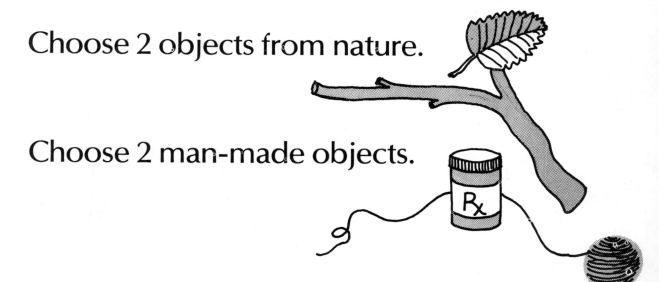

Choose 2 man-made objects.

Build something that an animal can use.

Tell a friend how it can be used.

Choose 10 things.

Some of these must be .

Some of these must be <u>straight</u>.

Build something that carries things.

Draw a picture of it.

Choose an equal number of
two different kinds of junk.

Build anything.

Describe it to the teacher.

Choose silver junk:

   2 shiny ones

   2 dull ones

   4 round ones

   3 square ones

Build a silver sculpture.

Put it on display in the office.

FIND AND FINISH

Find these.

a marshmallow

wood

Put them together.

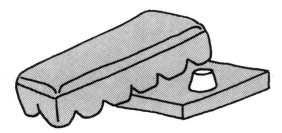

Finish it to make a scene for a story.

How old are you?

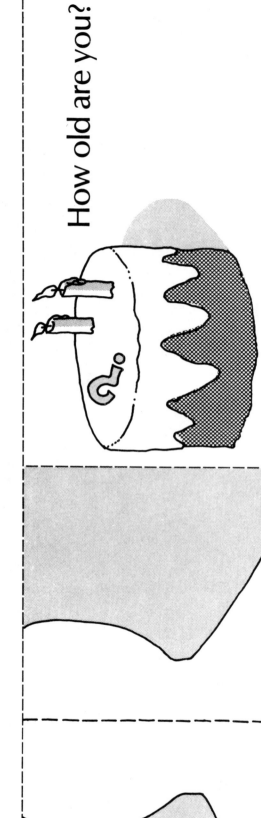

Put that many pieces of jewelry on your arm.

How old were you last year?
Put that many pieces of jewelry around your neck.

How old will you be next year?
Put that many pieces of jewelry on your ankle.

Dress	Dress
your	your
right	left
side	side
in	in
gold-	silver-
colored	colored
jewelry	jewelry

Put on as much jewelry
as you can in **5** minutes.

How long does it take
to take it off?

Have a jewelry race
with your friend.

To Your
Mark
Get Set Go!

Put some
jewelry on
above
your waist.

Put some
jewelry on
below
your waist.

Make a pattern with the letters in your name.

Make a pattern with

2 leaves

4 flowers

Sew on a pattern using buttons.

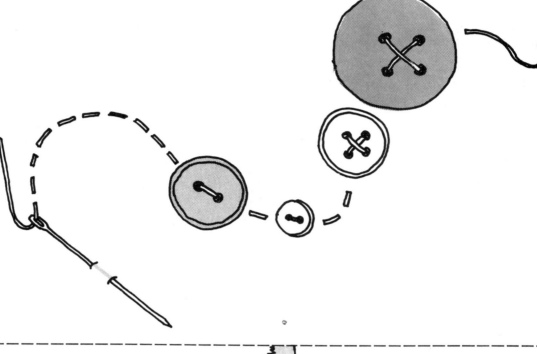

Make a pattern using

yellow

green

blue

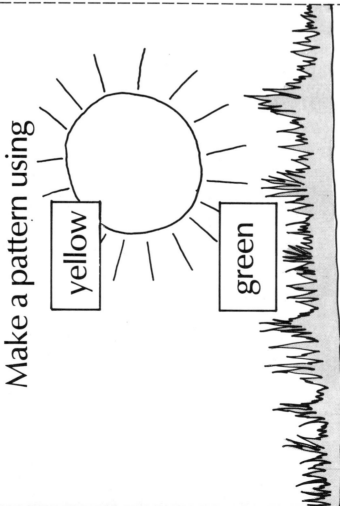

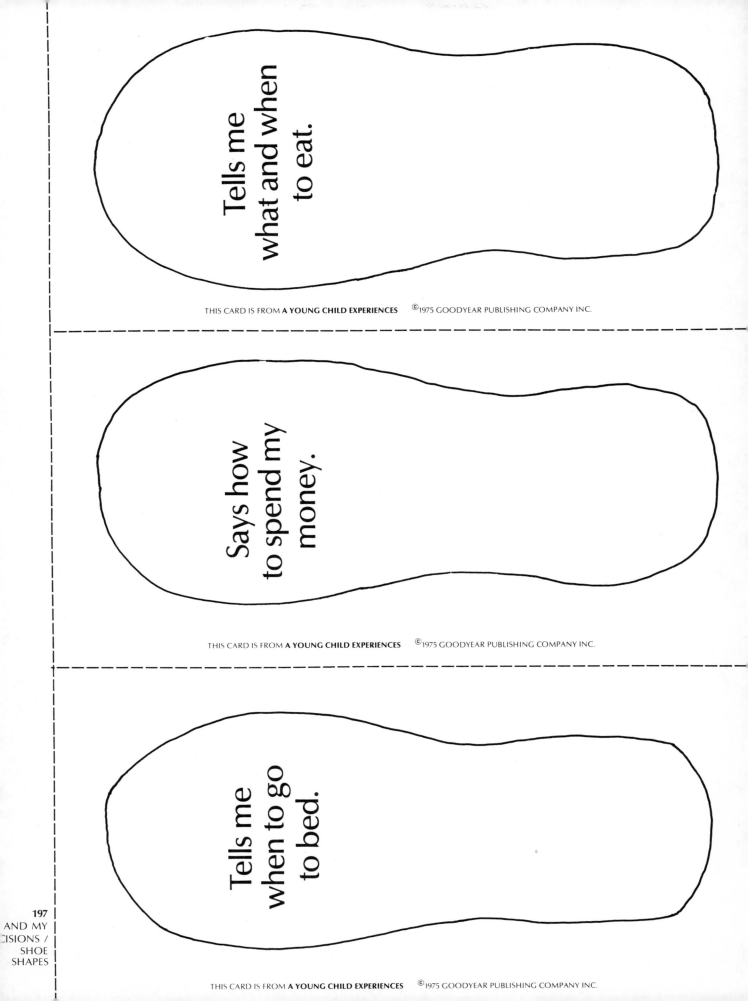

Tells me
what and when
to eat.

Says how
to spend my
money.

Tells me
when to go
to bed.

Chooses my clothes.

Ties my shoes.

Makes me do my chores.

Chooses
my
friends.

Chooses
new toys.

Decides
how I
wear my hair.

My order is:

MILE HIGH

4 scoops
on a triangle.

My order is:

BANANA
SPLIT

3 different
flavors on top
of a banana.

THIS CARD IS FROM **A YOUNG CHILD EXPERIENCES** ©1975 GOODYEAR PUBLISHING COMPANY INC.

My order is:

COLORFUL CALORIES

Make a pink sundae
in the dish.

Cover it with a pink sauce.

Label the kinds of
ice cream you used.

My order is:

SOUPY DISH

A melted
scoop in
a circle.

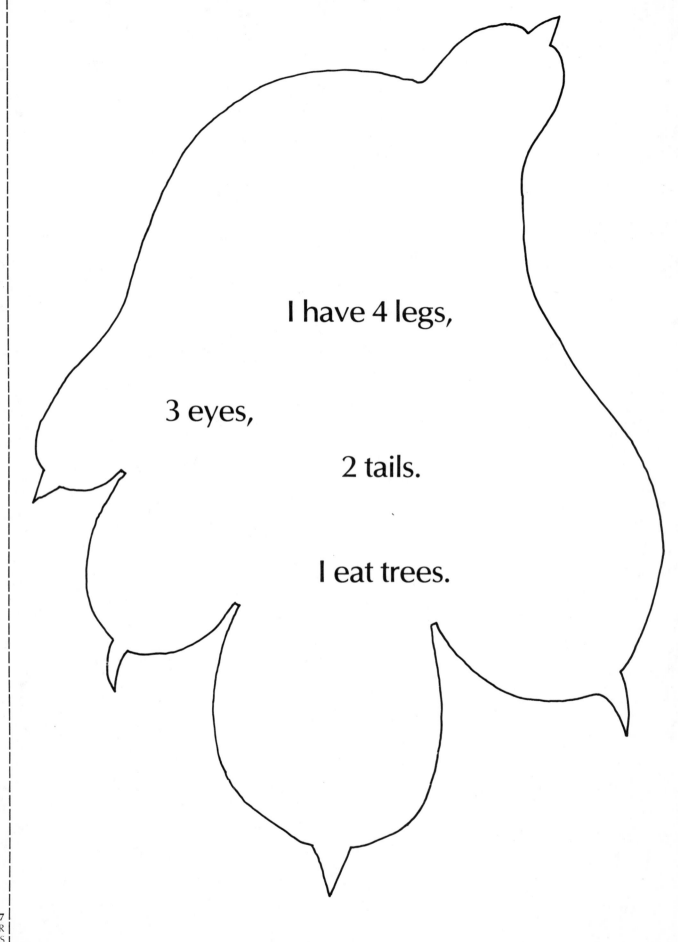

I have 4 legs,

3 eyes,

2 tails.

I eat trees.

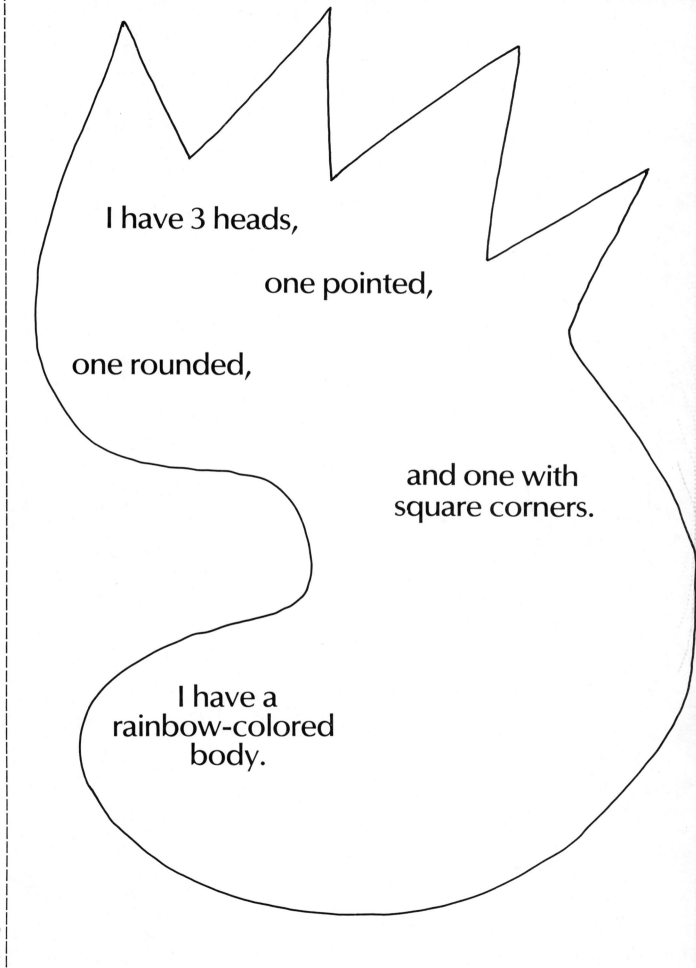

I have 3 heads,

one pointed,

one rounded,

and one with
square corners.

I have a
rainbow-colored
body.

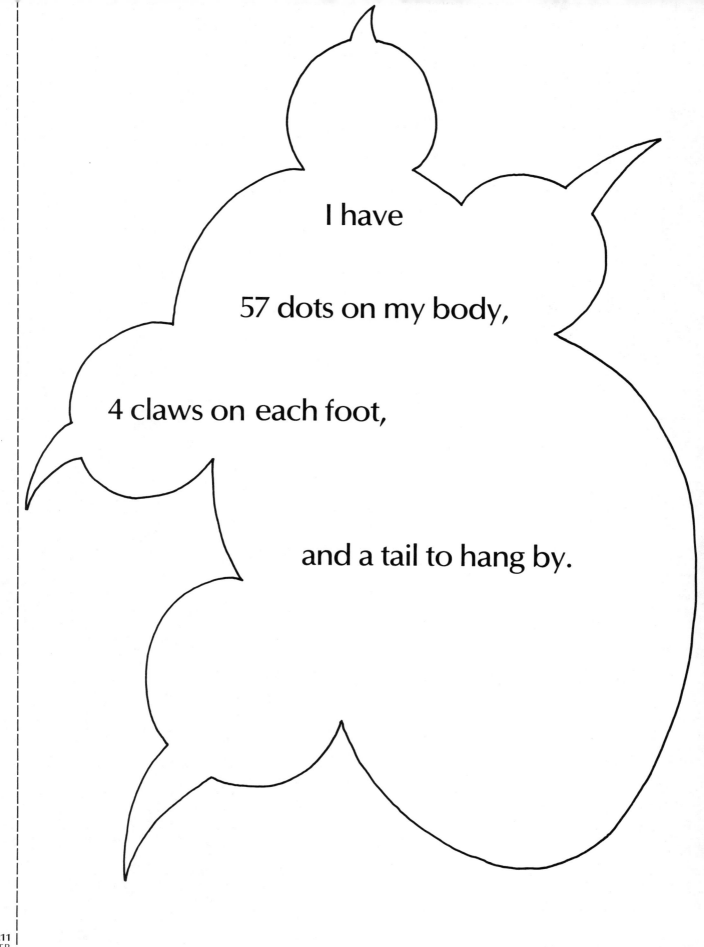

I have

57 dots on my body,

4 claws on each foot,

and a tail to hang by.

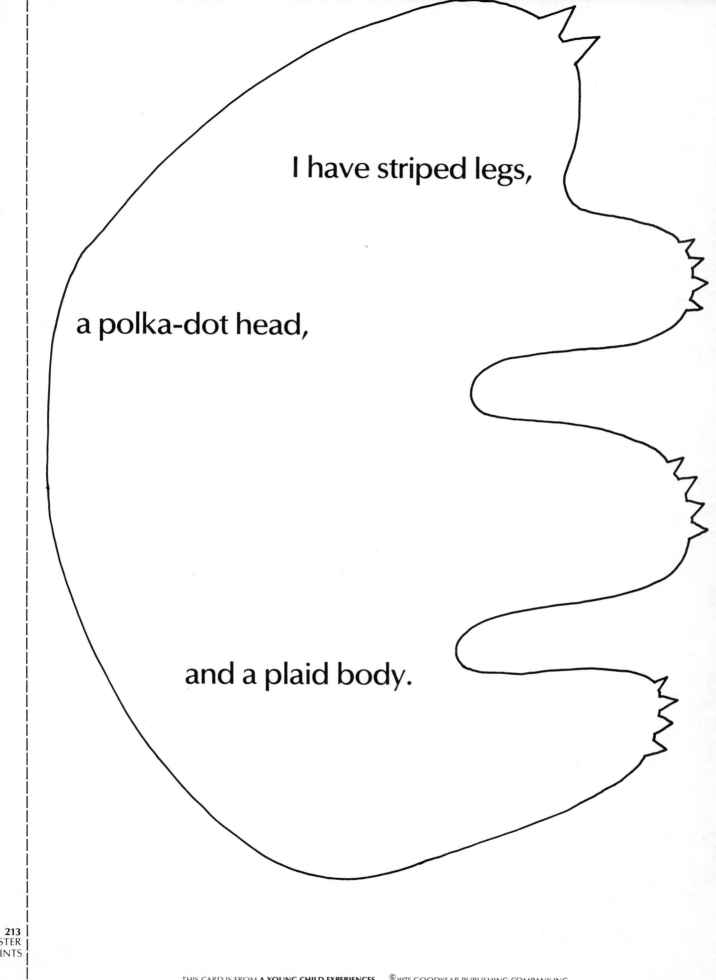

I have striped legs,

a polka-dot head,

and a plaid body.

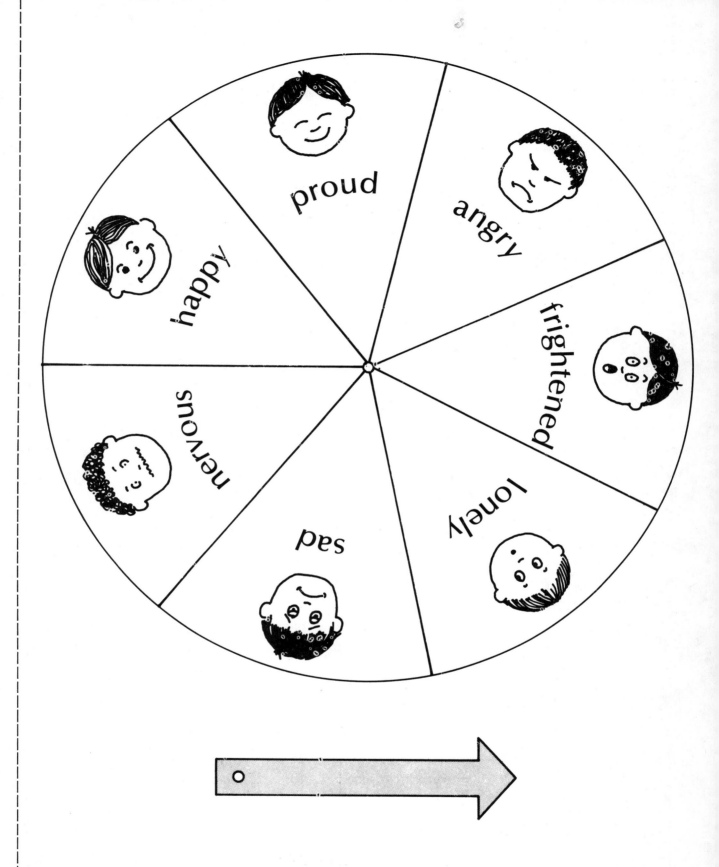

Attach spinner to the center of the circle to complete the game.

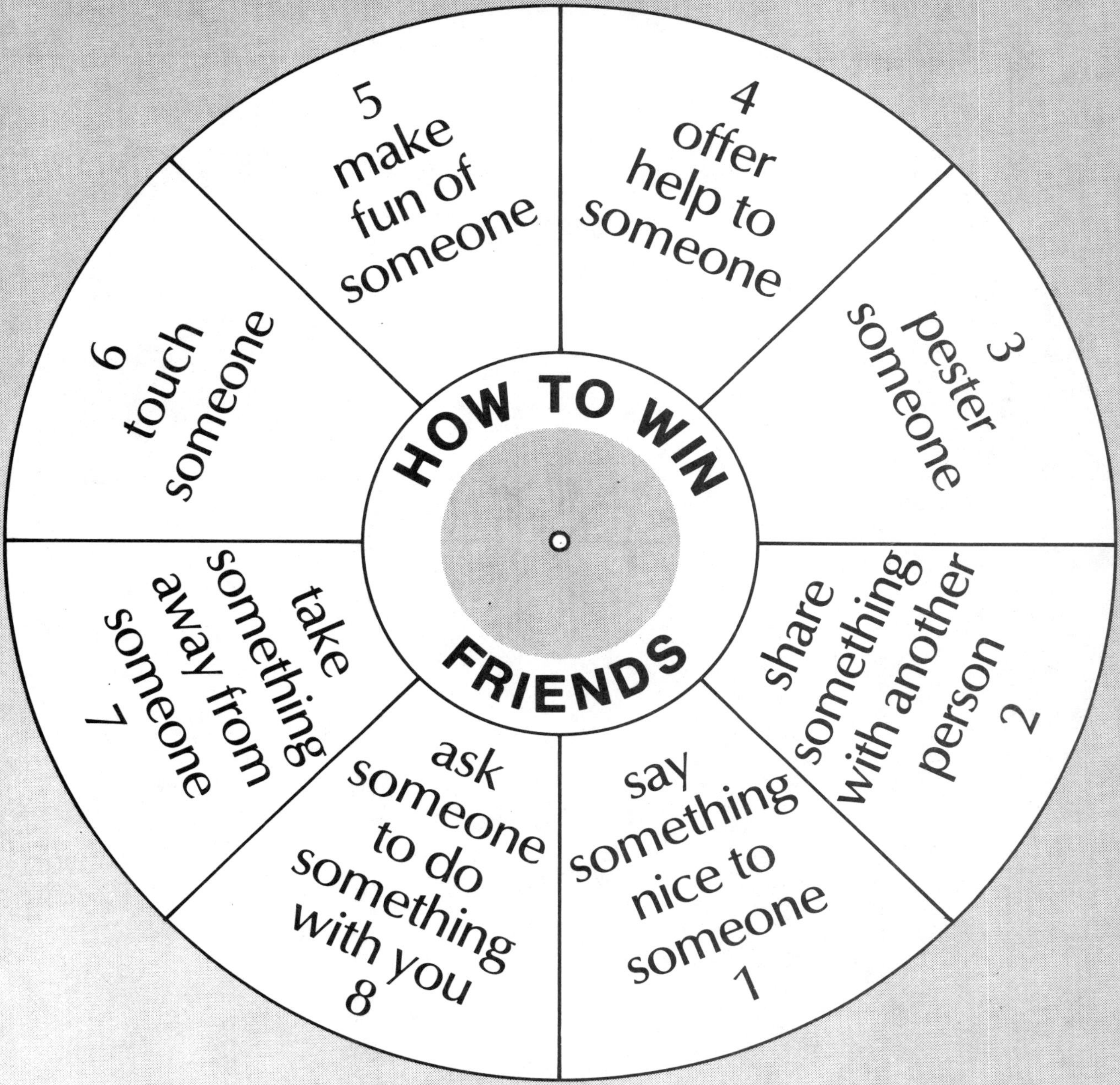
HOW TO WIN FRIENDS
1 say something nice to someone
2 share something with another person
3 pester someone
4 offer help to someone
5 make fun of someone
6 touch someone
7 take something away from someone
8 ask someone to do something with you

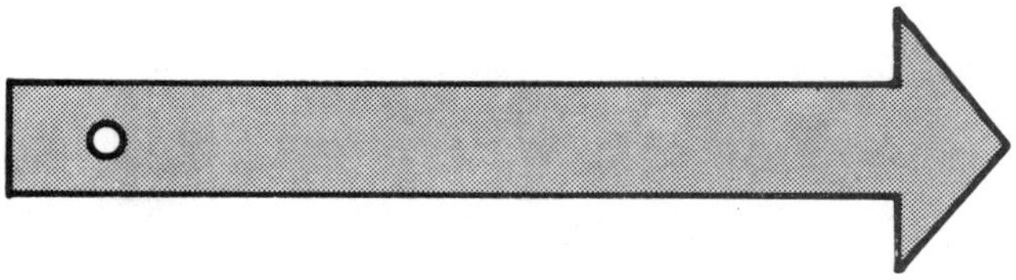

Attach spinner to the center of the circle to complete the game.

COLLECTOR'S HOUSE

Draw or name the piece of junk in the room where you found it.

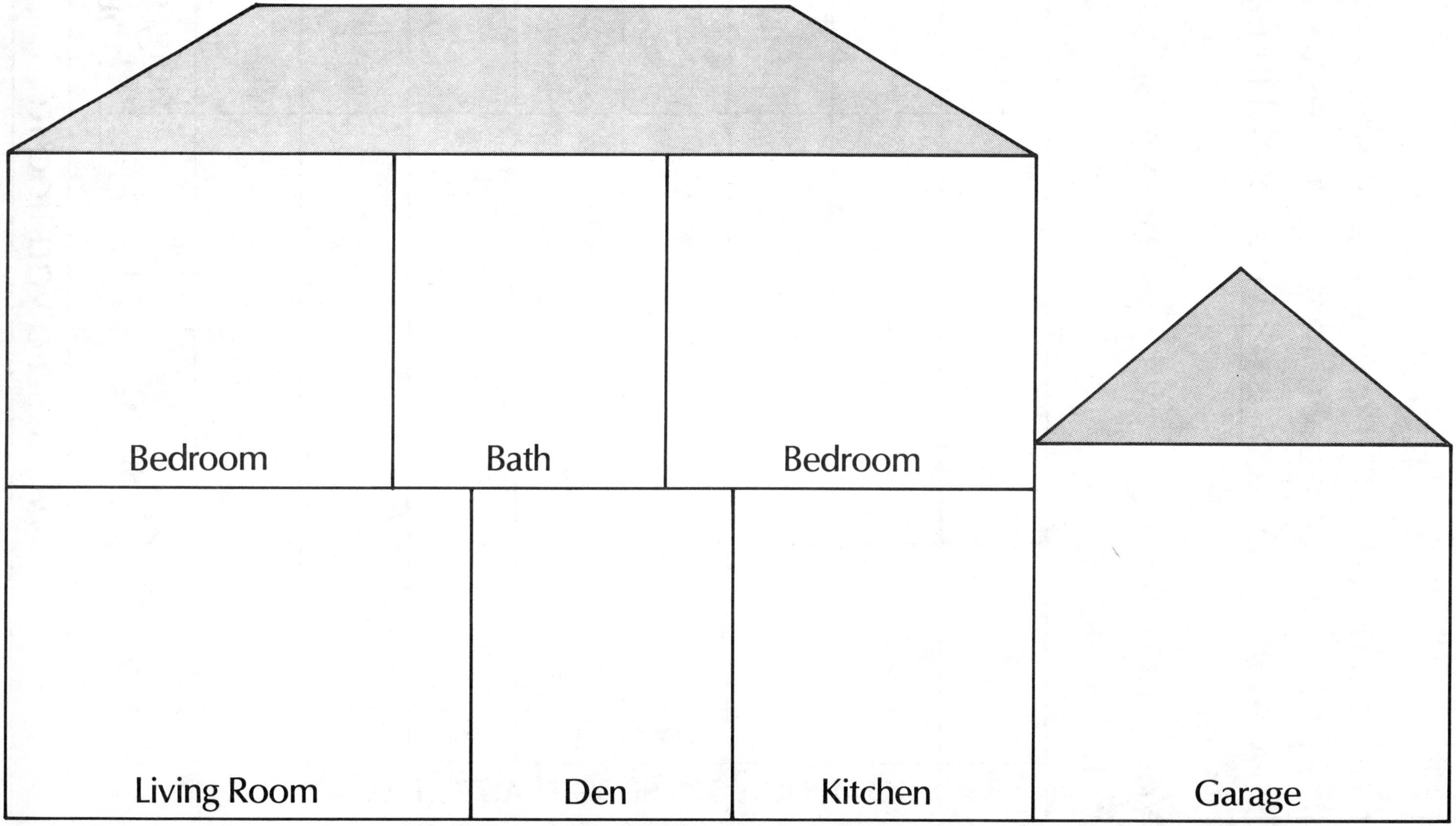

Bedroom

Bath

Bedroom

Living Room

Den

Kitchen

Garage

THIS CARD IS FROM **A YOUNG CHILD EXPERIENCES**   ©1975 GOODYEAR PUBLISHING COMPANY INC.

COLLECTOR'S GRAPH

Find the places on the graph that show where the junk was found. Fill in the squares to show how many pieces of junk you found in each place.

You can use colors, pictures, or symbols to fill in the squares.

How many pieces did you find?		yard	store	house	neighbor's house
5					
4					
3					
2					
1					
		yard	store	house	neighbor's house

Where did you find it?

THIS CARD IS FROM **A YOUNG CHILD EXPERIENCES**   ©1975 GOODYEAR PUBLISHING COMPANY INC.

What numbers describe you?
Fill in each part of the chart with the numbers
that tell about you.

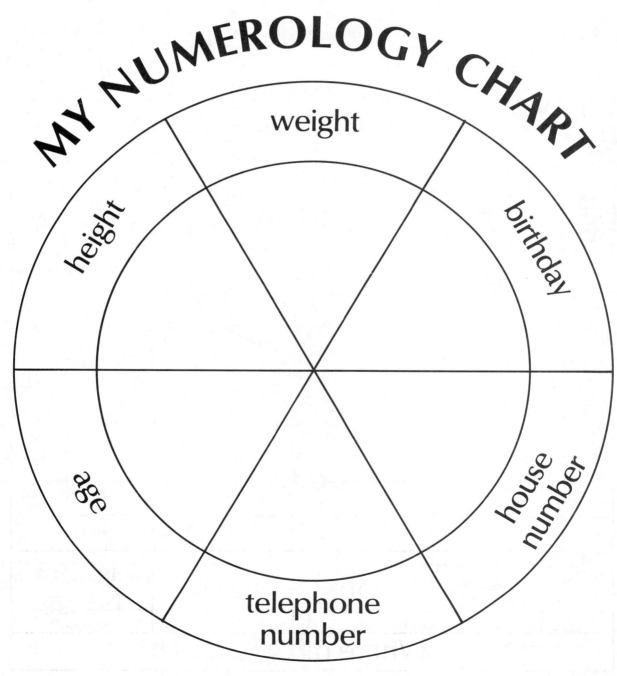

MY NUMEROLOGY CHART

weight

height

birthday

age

house number

telephone number

Cut out the arrows at the bottom of the page.
Read the situations on each of the arrows.
Glue each arrow on one of the circles in the
target to tell how you feel about the situation.

FEELINGS TARGET

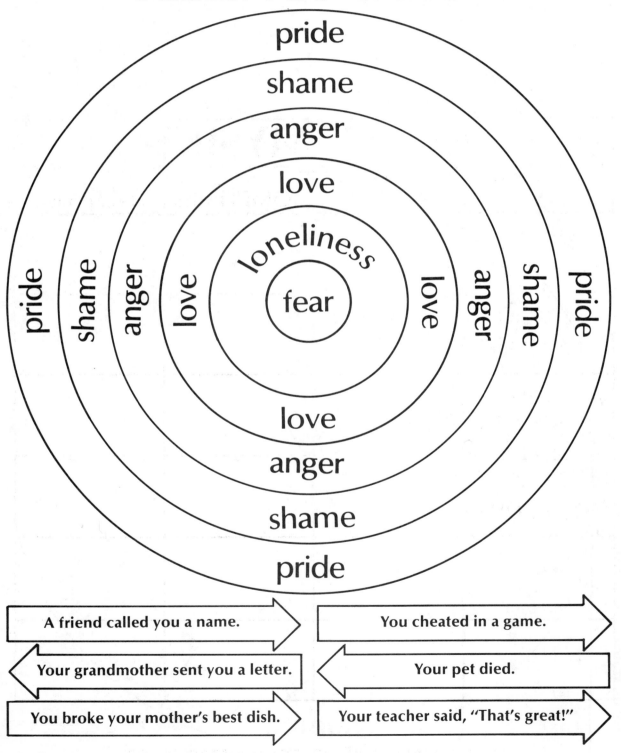

A friend called you a name.

You cheated in a game.

Your grandmother sent you a letter.

Your pet died.

You broke your mother's best dish.

Your teacher said, "That's great!"

Do you do these things by yourself?
Do you get help to do these things?
With your parents, check the box by each thing to show your answer.

ALL BY MYSELF			
	ALL THE TIME	SOMETIMES	NOT YET
get dressed			
comb my hair			
set the table			
clean my room			

223
I CAN
DO IT
MYSELF /
ALL
Y MYSELF

LETTER HOUSE

Each letter lives on different floors of the house.

How many floors of the house does this letter live on?

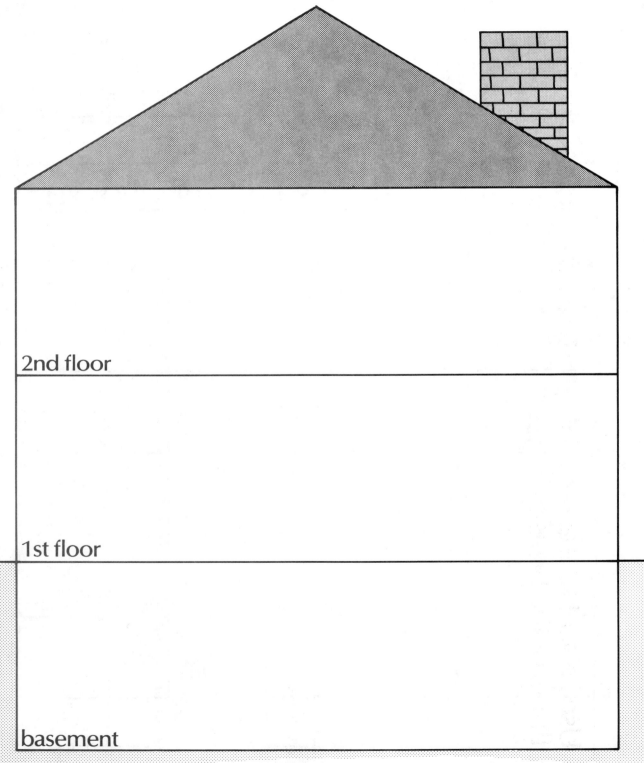

2nd floor

1st floor

basement

Use Letter Houses. Practice the letters by making them live on the correct floors of the houses.

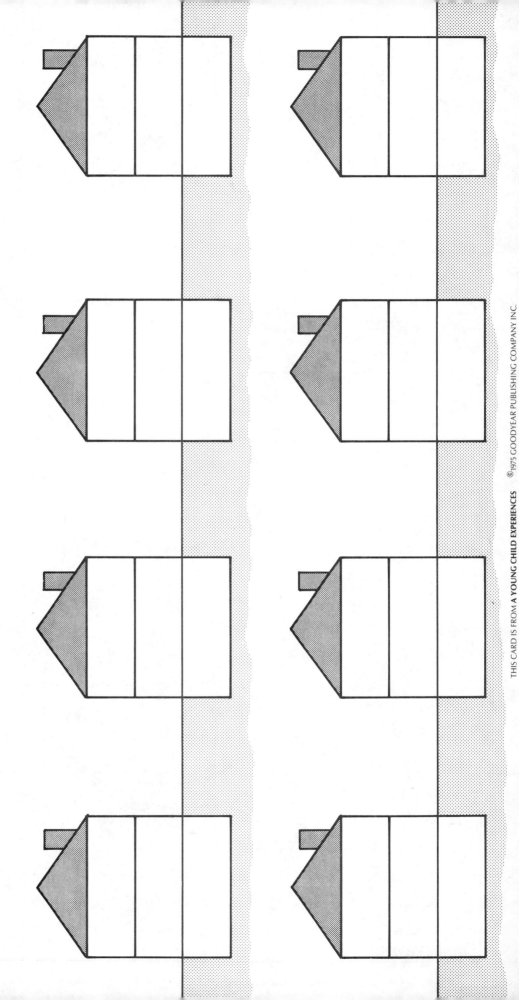

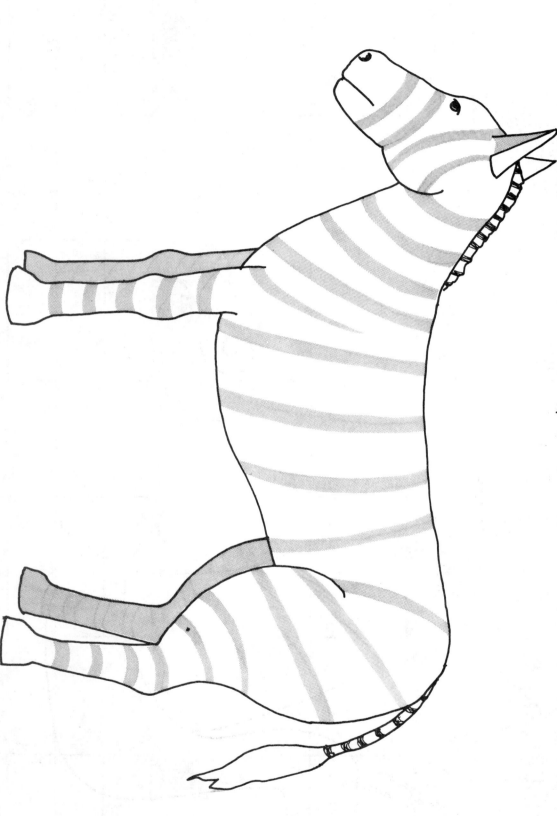

LINE LETTERS

Write the letters with lines like stripes inside the zebra.

CIRCLE LETTERS

Write the letters with circles inside the snail.

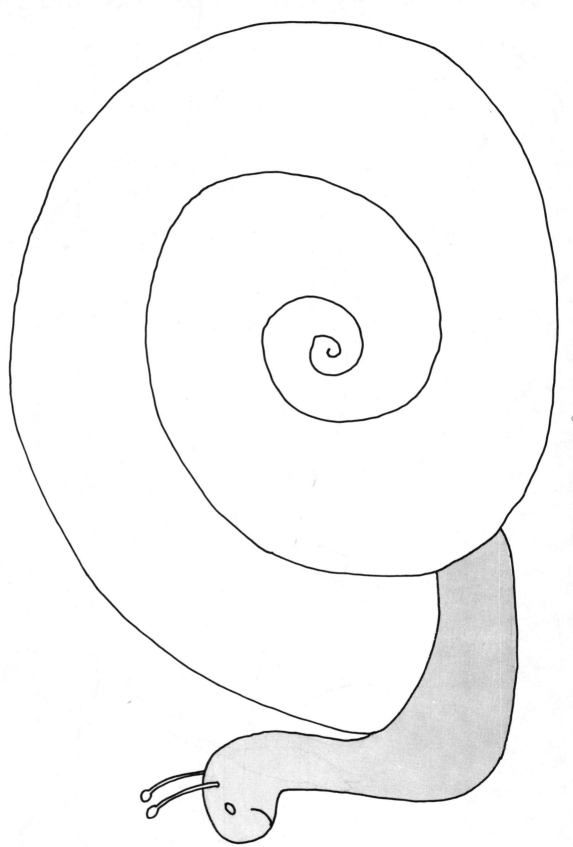

HUMP LETTERS
Write the letters with humps inside the camel.

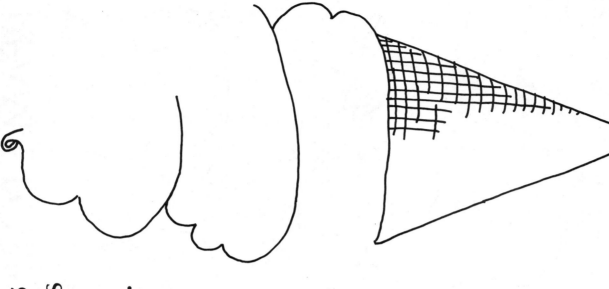

FINISH THE CONES

Draw in the lines to finish the ice cream cones.

Color one cone in fall colors.

Color one cone in vacation colors.

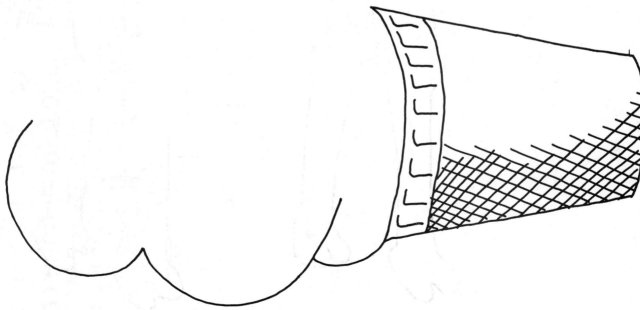

ICE CREAM STORE

Use the Ice Cream Store Chart. Fill in the ice cream cones on this page to match the chart.

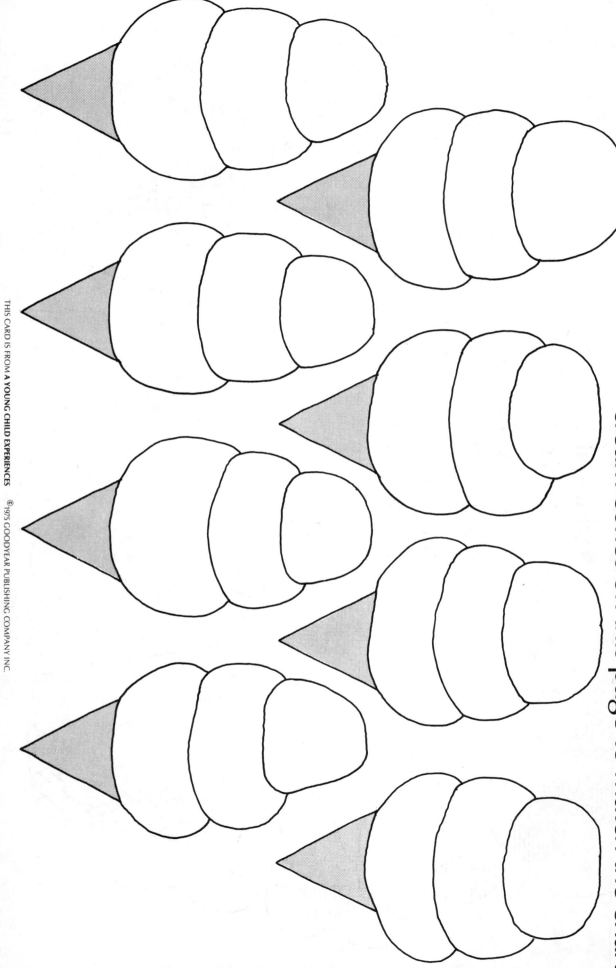

FLAVOR CONES
Rewrite each word so that all its letters are alike.
Use either all capital or small letters for each word.

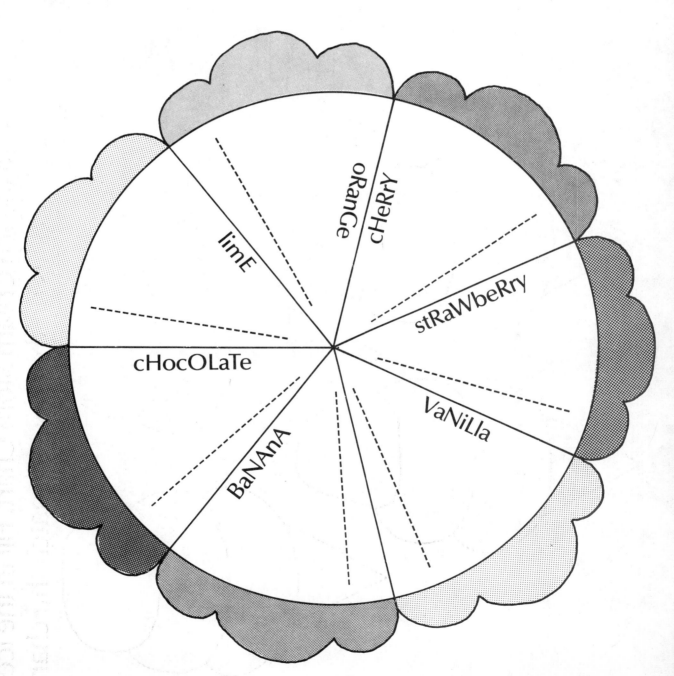

oRanGe

cHeRrY

limE

stRaWbeRry

cHocOLaTe

VaNiLla

BaNAnA